Disciple

Walking with God

RORISANG THANDEKISO

AS TOLD TO

Nkhensani Manabe

LUX VERBI

Edited by Glynne Newlands
Cover and layout by Natascha Olivier, Coco Design
Photos on cover and photosection: Andile Mthembu

LSiPOD: 978-0-7963-2400-9 (First edition, ninth impression 2025)
ISBN: 978-0-7963-2331-6 (epub)

In the year that King Uzziah died, I saw the Lord, high and exalted, seated on a throne; and the train of his robe filled the temple. ISAIAH 6:1

To my beloved friend Eva, I love and miss you dearly. Your passing overwhelmed me so much that the voice of God was the only thing I could hear; in my grief I could see nothing but the Lord, who sustained me. I pray that I will represent you well as I continue in our quest to go out into the world and tell people about Jesus.

And to my mother, Matai Karabelo Thandekiso, thank you for gifting me with Jesus.

Contents

Foreword

Rorisang is one of the greatest loves of my life and my biggest inspiration! She's my sister and my oldest friend. I adore her. Growing up she was confident, curious, bubbly and an especially kind child. From a young age, this vibrant girl knew that she wanted to be in entertainment so used to practise being on TV. When she landed a role on YoTV, I was not really surprised. What did surprise me, though, was how big and far-reaching TV is, and how it changed Rori's life.

From a very young age her faith in God was strong. She was the first person I witnessed who without a doubt lived out her faith, trusting that nothing is impossible with God if you believe. It was evident in her speech and in her actions. Rori has worked extremely hard to be where she is, walking boldly through every door that God has opened up for her, and sitting at every table to which she was invited. She's wasted no opportunity! It has been such an honour to watch her become the powerhouse she is and yet still remain true to herself, to see her pursue her dreams so relentlessly, and to witness how she intentionally takes other people with her as she rises.

I am confident this book will touch the hearts of many people across the world and that it will minister to their lives. I believe it's a book you will read more than once, and I'm excited to watch firsthand this part of her journey. Her story is so incredible yet so relatable. God's hand and call on her life have always been evident – He's been so kind! I am so proud of the woman she is and am continuously challenged by how deeply empathetic and generous she is towards strangers and kin alike, how she lives out her salvation.

May God bless you and keep you, Rori. I will love you until Tom catches Jerry! I'm so unbelievably proud of you!

BOKANG THANDEKISO

Foreword

Rorisang is a loving, kind and helpful child, a respectful daughter who is always ready to sacrifice for her family and friends. She embraces others regardless of their background, status or socio-economic factors.

She maintains a fresh outlook on life, and even when things are difficult, she continues to feel a sense of wonder and joy. She is always filled with a sense of gratitude, no matter what.

Rori is the kind of person who views life as it unfolds logically and rationally. She is not afraid of facing problems and actually enjoys using her problem-solving skills!

She has a sense of purpose – Rori knows that in this life, she has a specific mission, duty and responsibility that she must fulfil.

Love from MAMA

Welcome to my life

When I was very young and first learning about God, I wanted to be a disciple. To me, the disciples were the superheroes of the Bible.

As I grew up and learned more about what the disciples went through, I still had a deep respect for them, but also formed a more realistic view of them. "Well, the Bible has already been written, so I can't fit into the Good Book like I wanted to," I thought. But, more seriously, I learned that there were other ways for me to contribute to God's Kingdom.

I looked at the pillars of the fivefold ministry – Apostles, Prophets, Evangelists, Pastors and Teachers – and that gave me an idea of where I could fit in, even if I was not a part of the executive committee of a church.

I later realised that I could be a disciple in my own space: through debating, missionary work, and TV and radio work.

Wherever I was was where God needed me to be.

When I was first approached to write this book, I quickly realised that I wanted to talk about the way in which I had learned to put my faith into action in all aspects of my life. It is important to me because I have seen how we in the church can get caught up in focusing on one thing: we give to charity and say, "That's how I love"; we attend church on the right days, wear the right clothes, say the right things, follow all the rules in church and say, "I've got faith". But we seldom interrogate our motivations and intentions.

What I want this selection of stories from my life to highlight is the pride of place that God has in my heart. These stories have been compiled to illustrate both the depth of my relationship with God, and also the unending grace that is available to all who turn their hearts to Him.

In some way, I have always wanted to share, to love, to build community with God at the centre. This is not the first time I have put stories together: at university I started a book of what I will call "proto-testimonies": *What I wish they had told me.* I began with my own journal entry about how I wish I had known that losing my father to illness when I was still very young would leave me with a grief so deep that it came in waves for some time afterwards. I asked people on campus to share their stories; they spoke about career choices, relationships, family life. I knew that this compilation could do the important work of removing the feeling of isolation people experienced. I knew that coming together in community could cause a positive shift.

That collection never saw the light of day, but the seed was planted, and I believe the book you're reading now blossomed from that garden of ideas.

In these stories, I hope you find new perspective and renewed dedication to appreciating all the lessons in your life.

In my years on earth, I have lived a full life, which has afforded me the opportunity to know God, to explore my talents, and through work to travel, create and connect.

I believe I am an example of what can happen when you tune into the message that God has for you, and use that message to launch your life.

I am sharing these stories because my heart for people is full to overflowing. I want to share my life so that others can feel free to do the same: to go out, love openly and share their faith boldly.

Life as a Christian is not easy. Tests, trials, disappointments and challenges await us all. But that is all part of God's plan: God places you in situations so that you can draw nearer to Him and learn what He has in store for you.

The path through life is challenging but rewarding, and through these stories I hope to open your mind and heart to all the possibilities that await for someone who gives their life over to God.

The best thing
my mother
gave me

My love for God is the cornerstone of my life. From the time I was preaching to the children at my school, through to the mission trips and now with *Jesus This, Jesus That*, the evangelism project that God brought into my life, I have been unapologetic about my faith. I live out my convictions every day. No one who meets me can have any doubts about that!

Because I am clear about this, observing the many ways that other Christians downplay their faith to avoid conflict with people outside the church is distressing. Where there is faith, there should be no shame or fear.

In today's world, Christians are often asked why they believe, and the image of the church is under attack even from the inside. I have seen people striving to be accepted in society instead of standing up for the Word of God.

Because we as Christians try to be palatable to everyone, we focus on being agreeable, instead of being clear about where we stand. We don't give non-Christian people room to expand into our lives; we don't demand that they respect our beliefs and our boundaries.

Through experience, I have learned that trusting God and making decisions accordingly is the greatest reward.

Demonstrable acts of faith and worship raised me and made me into a person who excelled in all areas of life. Our upbringing was so rooted in Christ and Christian service that God and the church became the tangible atmosphere in which we developed our selfhood. There was no doubt about whose Word we lived by.

My mother turned to prayer at all times – it was as natural as offering a hug or reaching out a hand to lift someone up. Whenever you need help, pray. When you are grateful, pray. When you see others in need, pray – for them and for yourself. My mom would often call on me to pray when we were out visiting family or community members.

I couldn't get too lost in any teenage reverie before my mother would call on me to pray. I would often hear, "Rorisang, rapela!" Sometimes I'd feel as if my mother was picking on me – I mean, why was *I* being called to pray for all these strangers? – but what I realise now is that she was training a muscle.

I was in the *habit* of faith. During my school days, I would travel through the city in taxis, sitting in the back seat looking out the window and praying for the people I saw. The praying muscle was connecting with my heart for service and I would try to genuinely connect with the people I met.

My mother taught us the importance of tithing, emphasising that it was an offering that stood in the gap where God would do His work. For this reason, I valued money and the difference it could make. So, on my travels when I would come across people who needed financial help, I would try to give, but if I couldn't, I prayed for God to bring someone to them who had the means to be a blessing to them.

I was in constant conversation with God. As my mother had shown me, He was my confidante, adviser and guide to whom I could go in every situation. The environment in which I grew up continuously suggested that God was the answer. Continuously.

This is why I believe that there is no area of your life that God is not a part of. In everything I do, I ask myself, "Where is God in this?"

The confidence I have in Jesus Christ gives me the audacity to be truthful and unashamed in all my interactions. I know that the Holy Spirit always goes before me. And I am eager to share the insights I receive.

Sometimes there is the instinct to downplay or "lighten up" the message. I often think, "Should I tell my friend that the Holy Spirit told me to advise them to do X?", because I am conscious of being received in the "wrong" way. But ultimately it *was* the Holy Spirit who told me, so why should I hide that?

Again, it is that awareness of trying to be palatable. But I am not a people pleaser when it comes to my faith. That's why I will always share that I put God first – I have set that boundary and demand that everyone in my life respects it.

Jesus is the greatest gift that my mother gave me.

At home there was a reverence for God that coloured our whole world. We were raised to be people of deep, demonstrable faith. And my mother's example has been so strong, so consistent, that no one could ever say that she is not true to her faith.

The clearest example I can remember of this un-wavering faith is my mother's behaviour in the wake of a fire that destroyed our home.

When I was in Grade 8, a fire that started in our garage drove us out of the house in the early hours of the morning. My mother led us to safety, then gathered us in her arms to pray. My older sister, my younger brother, my mother and I stood outside while she prayed, thanking God for our lives.

There was no panic in her movements as she lifted our eyes to God in this moment of crisis. The reminder was of Psalm 118:24: "This is the day the Lord has made. We will rejoice and be glad in it." (NLT)

This day – with a fire destroying our home – was still a day to rejoice and be glad.

Fortunately, we could salvage some of our clothing and we got ready for school at a neighbour's house. My mother sent us off and, aside from the teachers at school checking up on us, it was just a regular school day. There was nothing to fear. No need to panic or worry. The only thing there was, and is, is God.

When I think about practising faith without pretence and hesitation, I think about that time in our lives and how my mother moved us through it. Her heart and her actions were completely focused on God.

At the moment of the fire, my mother taught us to do the opposite of the expected reaction, to do the higher thing. She was secure in God and prompted us to do the same. Life caught her off guard but she stood fast in the knowledge that God would see us through.

My mother loves – and lives – out loud. The impact of her actions is so far-reaching, both into her past and into our collective future. As children we saw this in the way she was able to create and cultivate community. My mother worked as a teacher for many years, having studied in QwaQwa. When we visited QwaQwa, a place where my mother has roots but no blood relatives, there would be so many families to visit. My mother would take us around her old neighbourhood and show us where she used to work and spend her time during her school years. We would meet old friends of hers who still remembered her well. What was interesting was that there were so many young people who had the same first name as my mother! She explained that she and her schoolmates (who later became fellow teachers) were very active evangelists in the community and were known for being on fire for God. Their impact was so deeply felt that some of those community members went on to name their children after my mom.

This respect that people had for her makes sense when I consider that she comes from a special generation of teachers who had a special reverence for the profession. They saw themselves not just as teachers but also as *educators* – as community builders. And that old-school approach put my mother in a perfect position to love and nurture all the children she came across in her classroom.

Her commitment to her work became clearer to me when one day, after fetching me from a doctor's appointent, she took me to school with her. In that classroom, I observed how connected she was with the learners and heard some of them calling her "mama". I asked her somewhat peevishly why this bunch of high-school kids would say that, but she told me to leave it alone, saying, "ke bana baka!"

And that was that: she was their teacher, but she was also genuinely invested in their wellbeing. Her heart for the community in which we lived showed in the way she would often take in learners in need, bringing them to live with us. We didn't ask how long they would be staying, and my mother would further involve us in helping by telling us to check our wardrobes for clothes to share with them.

I can imagine that it was difficult for a single parent to further extend herself and her resources in this way. I believe it speaks to her heart for Jesus, to how seriously she takes obedience and submission to the will of God. I think you have to really be in love with God, to be so secure in Him that you feel confident enough to make big moves on His behalf.

Extending kindness and being compassionate came naturally to my mother and gave us all permission to express our love for the community as well.

My mother lived her faith in a way that gave us, her children, licence to proudly claim Christ for ourselves. She has always had a bold faith: she lives out her Christian values in a big, proud way, letting her love for Jesus colour all her actions.

For me, she is the living example of the Scripture that says, "Train up a child in the way he should go …" (see Proverbs 22:6, NKJV). I consider myself properly trained up! The way in which I grew up in my faith is related to the submission and obedience that my mom modelled for us.

Her approach to life is also inviting: she has the ability to connect with and hold space for people, and they naturally return the favour. This is how my siblings and I came to have so many aunts and uncles who are not blood relatives. As black people, we already have an open and accommodating definition of family, quickly regarding friends as sisters and elderly neighbours as grandparents, but with my mother it feels slightly different.

The love my mother has shown to people in her life means that she has relationships with colleagues from the beginning of her career, and also with their children, and with the members of her church community, and with anyone she feels called to bring into her life. She will actively reach out to people – a phone call or WhatsApp is never too much – and sincerely check in, wanting to know how they are and how she can help.

All these people who she is living her life with are also important to me. And they will all be at my wedding! I often wonder what the balance will be like: I have uncles who are family relatives, and then I have all the uncles who have adopted me along the way, and all of them watched me grow up and are invested in my happiness and success.

My mother's example of love, family and community is so consistent that it naturally poured over into us and how we treated the people we came across.

I remember how I extended help – and our home – to a woman and her young child when I sensed that she was in need. Yes, my family and I were between homes and it was clear that we were struggling, but that did not stop me from showing love and compassion for my neighbour. That was the result of my mother's teaching.

It might surprise people to know that my mom is a bit of a "hippie". She has this open, free spirit and she loves talking to and connecting with people. She has a joyful heart and a playful attitude. My mother is one of my best friends. She enjoys clothing and fashion (always stealing my newest, coolest items before I even get to go out in them) and she loves to keep up with her favourite soapie, *Skeem Saam*.

When we were younger and still living at home, my mother infused playfulness into her parenting style. She made an effort to teach me nursery rhymes in Sesotho, using something fun to deposit important lessons from her own childhood into mine. I remember mornings spent play-wrestling with her and my sister, something that became a fun way for us all to spend time together. It is that quality time that allowed us to get close to our mother and listen to her stories about her life, which were also lessons for our futures.

Today, my mother is my favourite travel buddy and the person who teases me the most, especially about work or about getting recognised by people when we're out together. She'll call me a "celebrity" and has been known to poke fun at me with her version of the Cassper Nyovest and DJ Sumbody song "Remote Control", which is about instantly recognisable people and the fans who make them famous. She jokes because she loves me. And I suspect it's also her way of keeping me humble: I may be on TV sometimes, but I am still her daughter and I still have a duty to her and all my other people. She is proud of me but she will not let my success, whatever it may be, get to my head. If you ever get to chat to her, ask her how she threatened to confiscate my car – which I had bought with my own money – when I was about 21 years old!

She has a big heart but, more importantly, she is a disciplinarian, just like her father. I respect and love my mother so much and I am grateful every day for the way she has helped me to navigate life in this wild world.

Growing pains

Memories of growing up in my mother's house will always feature a few key things: discipline, love and fun. My mom is an example of that powerful archetype: the Black Parent in the Nineties. Black parents in the 1990s were a special breed. They approached raising children with a determination and strictness that fit the times: the world was changing rapidly – in popular culture, in politics, in technological advances. Everything was new and in some ways parents and children were discovering the world at the same time.

In this environment, my mother had three children to mould. Of course, she did not lean on her own wisdom. At the centre of all her parenting decisions was God, and the desire to raise us with the constant awareness and deep knowledge of Jesus in our lives. This showed through in the rules that my mom had for us: we were not allowed to go to sleepovers because she wanted us home, where she could watch over us; we were not allowed to take things from strangers because we didn't know where they came from and what their intentions were. We could only listen to certain music, and the TV shows we watched were vetted.

In the late nineties, shows like *Sabrina the Teenage Witch* and *Charmed* were new and popular. A show about a young girl who learns that she has supernatural abilities would be suspicious to most parents who had ties to the church, and Salem, the talking black cat that lived in Sabrina's home, placed the show firmly in my mother's "banned television" category. A black cat already symbolises darkness for people who are superstitious; one that can talk must surely be an instrument of the devil!

Charmed, a show about three sisters who lean into their powers as witches, was also a no-go. When we tried to explain to my mother that Prue, Piper and Phoebe were good witches, she said there was absolutely no such thing.

Things were the same with music. Around 2001, Destiny's Child released a music video for their hit song, "Independent Women Part 1". In the beginning of the twenty-first century, music videos had settled into the zeitgeist and were seen as big currency. We would come home from school to watch the latest visuals that artists created for their new music. One scene of the music video for "Independent Women Part 1" (which was the lead single for the *Charlie's Angels* soundtrack) showed Kelly, Michelle and Beyoncé standing back-to-back with their fists up in fighting stances, against the backdrop of rising orange flames. And, of course, that moment in the video would be the one when my mother walked in. Now that set alarm bells off in her head! No amount of explaining how the song is a rallying cry for women to stand up for themselves and take an empowered position in society could convince her that this shouldn't be banned from ever being played in our household.

How else would a Christian mother interpret an image of young women singing and dancing in a fiery room?

Music continued to be the site for a battle of wills. When Gerald Levert (may his soul rest in peace), then a successful American RnB crooner, was enjoying international airplay with his song "Made to Love Ya", it was also the height of that early 2000s fixation: the DIY songbook. Teenagers were plugged into entertainment and especially to music: magazines would print posters of popular artists and the lyrics of the songs of the moment, and teens would collect them and paste them into their own books of songs. Those who really wanted to show that they knew what was hot would listen to songs and write out the lyrics themselves. Memorising lyrics was how we shared pop culture.

Singing along to "Made to Love Ya", got me into trouble with my mother. When she heard me singing the chorus – "I was made to love you, my hands to touch you, my arms to hold you, my legs to stand, my time to spend with you forever" – she immediately nipped that idea in the bud. She made me read Psalm 139:14: "I praise you because I am fearfully and wonderfully made; your works are wonderful, I know that full well."

My mom was emphasising that my hands are made by and for God, my eyes are for God, my heart is for God ... She wanted to drill that into me, and steer me away from focusing on whatever imaginary lover Mr Levert was talking to. At the time I thought that she was being strict about nothing, but now when I think about it, I see how a mother would worry that her 12- or 13-year-old was fixating on an external love outside of the God who put her on this earth. It would feel as though your child could very easily lose their way and stumble into something terrible.

What my mom was trying to teach us is that what we listen to, what we watch, what we say are all very important in determining what we think and believe. It goes back to Romans 10:17: "Consequently, faith comes from hearing the message, and the message is heard through the word about Christ."

If hearing the Word brings faith, then it stands to reason that other things are brought about by hearing. By hearing, seeing and speaking, you are influenced, you are persuaded, and you are convinced. Your eyes and ears are portals.

This is also linked to how my mother, as a teacher, trained us to approach our school life. Homework was high priority and we had to participate fully in school life, always with the view of doing our best. We were encouraged to focus on our own work and to do our utmost, always with our classmates in mind – because we did have to fit into the school's environment, after all – but without letting their choices influence ours.

Anyone who has written an exam will be familiar with that feeling of "Did I do enough?" that comes over you when you walk into the venue and see other students studying (or rather cramming) material that you didn't spend time on. You start to feel like you read the wrong pages, begin to panic that you didn't study enough. And then you're unable to perform at your best.

In our house, my mother called this "academic suicide": by listening to what was going on outside, you ruined your chances at success; you broke down your faith in yourself. This concept was how my mother taught us strength in conviction: doing your work to the best of your abilities gives you the confidence to stand up and make your presence felt.

My mom's rules for us were strict, but they ultimately gave us a strong foundation from which to find and express our identity. This home environment made us into thoughtful, ambitious, caring people. And it made us into people who can appreciate the multifaceted nature of the human experience. My mother modelled full humanity for us, teaching us about discipline and dreams, vulnerability and joy. In many instances it all came down to joy, which we could freely experience because we had a safe home space.

Thinking about it now, I see that my mother's approach to raising us was geared towards giving us the full childhood experience. She was intentional and attentive and she always reminded us that we should enjoy just being kids. There was a separation of worlds – she was the adult and we were the children – and I believe it was important for her to keep that boundary in place, to ensure that we had a full childhood and didn't rush towards adulthood and all its problems.

This playful attitude would manifest in such things as the "hand tennis" games that my mother would play with us: with a tennis ball and some gumption, she would lead us in a game where the player with the ball had to bounce it while passing it under each leg alternately. I remember being surprised to see that she was so athletic!

Spending quality time with our mom taught us to value our relationship with her on multiple levels. She was a fun-loving person, but she was also (and always) our mother. We could engage on friendly terms but we also always knew where the line of respect was. That respect was for her, naturally, but also for ourselves and for the rules of society (that is: of the community at large that she was raising us to be a part of).

I remember learning about these rules of engagement from a situation involving one of the helpers my mother once employed.

At the time, my brother Ntlafatso was very young; he hadn't started nursery school but was just old enough to start stringing sentences together. Like his sisters, he was a curious, observant child. Whatever happened during the day when he was at home with Aus Maki, we would hear about it at some point. This is how Aus Maki got caught out!

Along with banning TV shows and curtailing our interactions with strangers, my mother also forbade dating. The kind of free socialising that was common in the early 2000s, where school children would have boy-friends and girlfriends, and these children could hang out at their parents' houses, was unheard of in our home. There were rules for engagement between boys and girls.

One afternoon, my mother came home earlier than Aus Maki would have expected her. If I were to guess, I would say that my mom had travel plans for the weekend and so she needed to leave work early. Well, what could have been a pleasant change of routine resulted in a family meeting.

For a while, leading up to that day Ntlafatso had been in the habit of kicking up a fuss whenever one of us would sit on a certain chair in the lounge. He would start crying and say, "No, that's Abuti's chair!" We had no idea who Abuti was but largely ignored Ntlafatso's fuss.

On that day, when my mother came home early, the mystery was solved. She walked in to find a young man sitting in exactly that chair that Ntlafatso was always protecting. This guest was clearly Aus Maki's boyfriend and he was used to visiting her while she was at work.

My mother greeted him, introduced herself and then later she called us children for a conversation along with Aus Maki.

She explained to us that in this family – because at that moment we were all part of the same family – we did not bring boys home unless things were serious. She said that who Aus Maki was dating was not our business and that the young man did not have good reason to feel comfortable in our home because he had not been formally introduced; he was not known to us as a man who was ready to start lobola negotiations or build a new family with Aus Maki.

It was inappropriate for him to be there, and while my mother would not dictate who Aus Maki could or could not see, she definitely enforced boundaries, letting us all know how things were going to go.

Making friends or dating was a part of life that we couldn't ignore, but we were being raised to interact within certain guidelines. What my mother was stressing during that slightly awkward conversation was the strict parameters where that could happen. She was encouraging us to use our discernment and good judgement – which she fully believed we had – to decide who to bring into the personal family fold when the time was right.

In that moment my mom was using her open yet firm approach to emphasise house rules, once again reinforcing a safe, stable environment in which we could learn new things about life.

After high school, when I left home to start university, I would commute between the Vaal and Pretoria. This quickly became unsustainable once I started at YoTV. I was attending lectures and then going to shoots that ran until well after 18:00 or 19:00, then getting into the car and driving home. By the time I got there I was exhausted and I couldn't properly participate in family life. I had to move out.

There was resistance from my mother, who did not see why I had to leave home. After the initial denial, my mother decided to write up a contract that she needed me to sign if I was to leave home.

This contract included stipulations about coming home regularly, contacting my family often, and behaving in a way that would honour them when I was out in public. By signing it, I promised to be disciplined, to remember where I came from, and to always uphold family values. It sounds somewhat reasonable now, but at the time I felt like my mother was being incredibly harsh and that she was holding me back. It was excruciating, because I also felt that she didn't trust me to be on my own, despite the fact that I had been doing so for some time already.

With time, I have come to realise that for my mother, my moving out felt like I was turning her world upside down: I was the first child to leave home, and I was following a path that she had no experience with. She didn't know how to protect me, so she took it back to what she had relied on before: rules and discipline.

Of course, I soon realised that none of the promises I had to sign my name to were far-fetched or unreasonable. Once you're away from home and you take on all the responsibilities of work, it is very, very easy to fall into the habit of neglecting your family. You start to move visits home further and further down your to-do list until you find you're only seeing your people two or three times a year. That's the kind of thing my mother was trying to prevent. She felt the separation deeply, even before it happened.

I remember calling one of my aunts who lived in Johannesburg and pleading with her to reason with my mom, to explain to her that I needed to take this step. We did not see my moving out in the same way and so for a while there was this rift, this misunderstanding in our relationship. It was a difficult time.

The issue with moving out was also related to how my mother did not fully understand my work. It was only after I took her with me on a full day of producing and presenting, travelling from set to set, that she got a clearer picture of what my life was like at work. She saw me stepping into multiple roles, creating television, and at the end of the day said, "I am exhausted!" For the first time she had a front-row seat to what was taking up my time and energy every day. She started to understand that although it wasn't one continuous contract, what I did was more than a "piece job", as she had previously referred to my work.

That day on set was maybe two or three years into my career, and after that day I feel that the friction between us finally started to ease. There was a new sensitivity from her that I hadn't seen before. Today, my mother is interested in everything I do, and is known to cut out clips from newspapers that mention me and my work. She has a box at home overflowing with my milestones; she's my biggest fan.

And for my part, I've upheld that important family value of quality time: I often drive home on a Saturday morning to spend time with my mother and my sister, giving myself the option to drive back just as soon as it gets dark. That's the beauty of living one hour away from home. But what's even better is that I do it not out of obligation but out of genuine concern for my family and because I truly do enjoy spending time with them.

The Bible is my daily guide

In Grade 4, I hit a roadblock in my education. Due to a long record of demerit points, which at Milton Primary School meant marks docked off school work, I was faced with failing the year. I was a good student, curious in class and diligent with work. But I was also a renegade, if you will.

At that time, schools were integrating and I was becoming more aware of race issues. I would not hesitate to pipe up and point things out; I was always pushing for justice. I remember the principal, Mr Booysen, once called me a "little Winnie Mandela" when I was only in Grade 2!

I loved people and knew how to hold their attention while I made speeches. I always had something to say – so I was always in trouble with my teachers. In the principal's office, my mother was presented with two options: take her child out of the school, or have me repeat the grade. I was a problematic element that they no longer wanted to deal with.

At home, my mother considered what to do about this obstacle so early in my academic career. Later, she spoke about taking the issue to my grandfather for advice.

"You are not taking her out of the school. If you take her out of the school, you are muting her forever. You are teaching her that she doesn't have a right to say anything."

My grandfather's main concern at that moment was with my voice in the world. He could see that if this disappointment was not processed appropriately, it could send a message that I would always be rejected for speaking my mind.

So, all my guardians decided that the best thing for me to do was repeat Grade 4. As a child, I couldn't see that vision. All I knew was that I would be spending another year in the same grade as a consequence for behaviour that I did not believe was wrong.

My mother, in a further example of how community was the cornerstone of her parenting style, called my aunt in for backup. It was time for them to highlight the way forward for me, and that way was Jesus.

I had just been served a big upset at school, I didn't know what the future looked like (well, as much as a 10-year-old can have a concept of the future), and what did my mothers do? They had me open the Bible and recite verses. I was repeating a grade, and my mom and my aunt had me reading Scripture! How about that?

> I can do all things through Christ, who strengthens me … (Philippians 4:13)

> Greater is He that is in you, than he that is in the world … (1 John 4:4)

The point they wanted to make is that no problem in my life could be beyond or above faith. And in terms of fighting for my place in school, the truth was, according to my mother, "only God qualifies you". My mother was teaching me that I can always speak up, but I have to learn *how* to do it.

Later in my school career, I fell in love with debating and I have no doubt that it was this incident that planted the seed. My love for speaking and sharing opinions was refined through debating and school, and those skills certainly carried over into my career in media.

In a world where people – black girls, especially – are constantly told to "tone it down", I realise now that my parents did the right thing in reinforcing that God-led confidence in me at a young age. On a practical level, the Grade 4 incident prepared me for high school and all its challenges.

When I started high school in 2005, the education system was in the thick of post-apartheid integration. Riverside High was a predominantly Afrikaans school that had just opened up to black learners and black teachers. There was a lot of movement in the curriculum and in the general operational style of schools.

We were among those schools piloting the RCL (Representative Council of Learners) system, which was an opportunity for learners to participate in leadership programmes at school and at provincial level.

In Grade 8, learners voted for their representatives and I landed in the top six: the Executive. At the beginning of high school, you're low in the pecking order. No one expects you to be prominent, especially not among senior learners. But somehow I was the exception.

So, there was a dilemma: my schoolmates had chosen me to represent them, but that would make me the only junior on the committee. How could I have a level of authority that is usually given to a matric student?

The principal suggested a compromise: I would have all the privileges and duties of the senior RCL members and I would be in charge of planning and running the junior assembly with the Grade 8s and 9s. I would get my RCL colours for the year, but my name would not go on the board in the hall as part of that year's Executive Committee.

There I was, the "outstanding student", drawing more attention to myself among a school of excitable teens. As everyone knows, the ones who stand out get singled out. This was when I began experiencing teasing and bullying from children at school. They saw my difference as a weakness and would always say things to remind me that I did not fit in.

I would come home from school in tears because I just could not get the teasing to stop. Before it could truly break my confidence, and as a strategy to remind me of who I was, my mother sent me to the Word.

To wipe away the tears, there were Scriptures. I remember my mother sending me to my room with a list of verses. She sat in the lounge, from where she could see into my room, and waited for me to recite the verses.

Over and over, until she was satisfied that I was loud enough and that I truly understood what I was reading. Those Scriptures became the script in my mind and heart. My mother was making sure I remembered who I was – *whose* I was.

Psalm 139:14-16 says, "I praise you, for I am fearfully and wonderfully made". Through this I learned and believed that there was nothing the bullies could take away from me.

That practice of repeating verses to myself when I feel challenged has stayed with me. Every day I turn to my Bible and know that I can be strong because I have divine guidance.

Let's talk about the virginity thing

In Grade 8, Mrs Mavimbela was my Life Orientation (LO) teacher. I remember her as a beautiful, warm-hearted woman. She cared about her learners and made it easy for us to talk to her about anything that was on our minds.

That year, 2004, saw the early and rapidly growing popularity of the Silver Ring Thing movement. During this time, groups of young Christians worldwide were declaring their commitment to abstaining from sex until marriage. The Silver Ring Thing was an organisation that travelled all over the world spreading the Gospel, engaging with youth on issues of faith, purity and commitment.

As a teen who was steadily building a strong faith in God and determined to walk the path, I also had one of these rings. Representatives from the Silver Ring Thing had come to our church's youth conference to sponsor us with Bibles and to give us an opportunity to purchase a ring and make a pledge. I bought my ring, signed the pledge, and was eager to make this public declaration of my commitment to walking with Christ.

In school, jewellery is not an accepted part of the uniform. (Ask anyone how teachers curbed their self-expression by taking away necklaces, and you'll have a full afternoon of conversation.) When Mrs Mavimbela saw my ring and asked about it, I explained to her about my vow of abstinence. I took the ring off, too, not wanting to enter into a larger discussion.

But Mrs Mavimbela had already seen an opportunity.

At the time, South Africa's public health communications were thriving. Television dramas, radio spots and talk shows were talking about the ABCs: abstain, be faithful, condomise.

As a teacher charged with equipping young learners with important life skills, Mrs Mavimbela decided to use my silver ring as an example of the right thing to do. Before I knew it, my LO teacher had planned for me to stand up at the next assembly and talk about my reasons for abstaining from sex.

Can you imagine what kind of pressure that puts on a teen? I was already accustomed to speaking in front of crowds, but this was a much more personal subject matter.

My mother was not impressed that this plan had been made without her. "Why didn't your teacher come and speak to me about this?" She could see the potential for things to go awry.

I stood up at senior assembly and spoke to my schoolmates about why I was not going to have sex until I was married. After that, there wasn't anyone in the school who didn't know about my purity ring. On the playground, that was the only conversation. Boys would ask me outright, "So, how far do you go?" It made things slightly awkward between me and my boyfriend at the time. I valued his friendship and I feared that drawing so much attention to him would cause embarrassment. He would be under scrutiny from his peers. Thankfully, he and I understood each other and he assured me that there was nothing to worry about. He was on his own faith journey.

Thinking back on how the assembly incident played out, it occurs to me that in that moment Mrs Mavimbela had placed me in a precarious position. As a high-school teacher and a parent, she was well aware of how volatile the school situation can be, and how children can latch onto things and twist them into something negative. She left me exposed, and it could have turned out very differently.

By the grace of God, the incident passed and left me with a stronger confidence in my convictions and in my voice. As Romans 8:28 says, "And we know that in all things God works for the good of those who love him …"

What that speech in assembly did was prepare me for my work in media. No scrutiny, name calling or questioning and criticism about my virginity and my faith could affect me negatively because I had dealt with all sorts of teasing at school.

When you work in the public eye, you're exposed. I learned how to deal with that at a young age.

A similar "exposure" happened later in my life when I was given the opportunity to speak as one of the guests on *3Talk* with Noeleen Maholwana-Sangqu. It was a Women's Day show and the segment that would cause the controversy was about "what women want".

Naturally, conversation turned to relationships and sex. When it was my turn to contribute, I explained that I didn't have anything to add because I was a virgin. Noeleen and the guests were surprised to hear this and it became obvious that some did not believe me.

I did not believe I had said anything remarkable; I had simply shared a part of my faith journey. But in the weeks that followed, and even up to this day, I was asked about my virginity. Why was I staying a virgin? Had I truly never had sex? How far did I go with men? People began to associate me with the purity movement and asked questions that ranged from the curious to the invasive.

All the while, I held on to what was true: my faith and my determination to follow Jesus. The relationship I had with Him was the most important thing.

The soundbite that stuck was "purity is possible". The way that people latched onto it, turning it and me into trending topics, showed me that there *are* people who want guidance in that area of faith. But it also showed me that there are people who spend all their time looking for someone to berate and break down.

After the *3 Talk* interview, the people I worked with also weighed in. Seeing the perception that colleagues and industry mainstays had about me and my faith showed me that everyone wants information about how to walk the path – and that many are under the impression that working in media does not align with being Christian.

But what I also saw is that people respected me and my decision, and would call on others in our company to do the same. Working on radio with the likes of HHP and ProKid, I found that they would take it upon themselves to play my protective big brothers.

Whenever the topic of my virginity came up, they would temper the conversation, steering it away from me and how I had decided not to have sex, rather encouraging people to see the good in the decision instead of meeting it with morbid curiosity.

It amuses me to see the headlines updating each year: *"Rorisang Thandekiso, virgin at 25"*, *"Rorisang Thandekiso, 30 and unmarried"*. People are counting down to … I don't know what!

What remains true in all of this is God. In the world, I am proud to uphold this discipline, which means I am destined for something much greater in the Kingdom of Heaven.

———

Dating as a young Christian woman does present some challenges. I am a spiritual being having a human experience, which means I always have to guard against leaning too much into worldly ways.

Thankfully, I had the kind of upbringing that reassured me of my identity and made me into someone who has strong boundaries, and is not afraid to state them. I learned this by example from my older sister, Bokang.

As the firstborn child, she was the one who modelled discipline for us who followed. All my mother's teachings about a Bible-led life were practised by Bokang first. She was our example, and I looked up to her.

When I finally started high school I was excited to be a part of her world. But, as any older sister would do, she quickly (but lovingly) threw water on the flame of my enthusiasm. On the first day of high school, we were in the taxi together on the way to Riverside High. When we got there, my sister handed me a note.

"I got through high school without failing a class, drinking, doing drugs or having sex. I expect the same from you. No excuses."

That was a reality check. I was in "big school" now and, while I was a good student who enjoyed new environments and people, I realised that this was a whole new ball game.

Later in life, as I went on to start university, meet new people through work and even more abroad, I continued to strengthen my boundaries and communicate them with the same respect I was demanding.

Self-discipline allowed me to see that even if I was getting to know someone who wasn't on the same faith journey as I was, I could freely state my intentions and let honesty lead the way. From early on, I did not romanticise dating and relationships.

I like the concept of a probation period. Think, 90-day rule. When I meet someone who expresses an interest in dating me, I tell them to put me on probation. Let's assess our compatibility by spending time really getting to know each other and learning each other's way of life.

Then they can decide if they are capable of being in a relationship with me.

In that probation period, I am upfront about who I am and how I approach romantic relationships.

When it comes to the question of virginity, I lay all my cards on the table very early on. Yes, I am a virgin. Yes, I am waiting for marriage. No, this is not going to change just because it's you.

To young Christian people asking themselves, "When is the right time to tell them I'm waiting?", the answer is, right away. Why wait? Your Christianity is core of who you are and there is nothing to gain from hiding it or putting it aside when you're dating.

Those who find the truth about dating you uncomfortable are not the ones for you. Okay? Okay.

It's more than church to me

Evangelism was part of my life from when I was a very young child.

My mother and the church community have a strong friendship and share family values. The "aunties" and "uncles" were our parents, too. If any of them stood up at my wedding to support and represent me, it would not be strange. Their proximity and familiarity made us all much closer than just members of the same congregation.

Growing up in a small town, church becomes small.

When your mother is heavily involved in the church, so are you. My mother was part of the intercession team, so we children were often at church outside of regular service hours. And we didn't do the simple children's church, either. We were right by our parents' side during all the work they did.

I was so engaged in church life that I was constantly looking for more to learn and more to do. I was attending Sunday School but, by the time I was about 12 years old, I no longer felt fulfilled there.

So, I decided to graduate myself! I remember saying to my mother, "I don't want to be in Sunday School any more". She reminded me that I still had two years to go before I could join the adults in the main service.

But I had already outgrown those classes. When we finished singing at Sunday School, before the main lesson would start, I would sneak out and go to "big church". When my mother found out, she again told me that I should stay with the children.

One day, the pastor, Moruti Jansen, found me lurking in the main church and asked if I was really ready for the responsibility of church. If I sat with the main congregation, would I pay attention and take notes? I confidently said yes.

The following week, the pastor announced that I would be joining the adults for that service, drawing attention to me and to my mother, who had no idea of my conversation with the pastor. Once again, I was Rorisang the maverick, bringing my mom more surprises with my decisions. I have been the "mischievous" child all my life.

Moving to the main church was a natural next step for me. Bokang and I had been on missions and taught the Bible. Having to go back to rudimentary lessons at my home church was frustrating. I needed more!

In my mind, I was far ahead from what they were

doing at Sunday School. On missions we'd go and teach the Word of God, visit people's houses, sit with grannies, clean for them and share the Word with them. Back at Sunday School, they were still doing memory verses.

During my first mission trip at the age of 12 or 13, we participated in building a physical church. Between the ages of 12 and 16, Bokang and I went on about six mission trips, mostly planned to coincide with the June-July school holidays. We would go through training on weekends, where the organisers of the missions would teach us how to approach new people, how to show respect for the communities, and the best way to present our message.

My muscle for teaching, for evangelism, was strengthened during that time.

On mission trips you witness miracles; I'm talking about things such as seeing a baby take their last breath and then come back to life. It strengthened my faith, and there was very little anyone could do to change my mind. And at the same time, it became evident that I needed to be fed more of God's Word. A growing mind and soul simply must be nourished.

I was also teaching Sunday School at Sonderwater, a neighbouring community where my church was doing outreach work. At one point I was attending three church services every Sunday with my sister. My mother tried to get us to cut back but soon realised that nothing would deter us.

I think the refrain in those days was "I want more". I had this eagerness to talk and teach about God, sharing love. Now I look at how *Jesus This, Jesus That* is the latest iteration of that work, and smile about how God has kept the passion for evangelism burning in me all this time. And it is something that came to me in a very strange way.

One day I felt compelled to post a screenshot of a Bible verse onto my Instagram page. It was 1 Corinthians 1:27-31: "But God chose the foolish things of the world to shame the wise; God chose the weak things of the world to shame the strong. God chose the lowly things of this world and the despised things – and the things that are not – to nullify the things that are, so that no one may boast before him. It is because of him that you are in Christ Jesus, who has become for us wisdom from God – that is, our righteousness, holiness and redemption. Therefore, as it is written: 'Let the one who boasts boast in the Lord'."

It's a Scripture that is familiar to people who have been raised in the church, but it's not necessarily one that would land for people who are not reading the Bible. Nevertheless, I felt compelled to post it on my timeline. I had no plan or agenda, and went to bed that night not thinking about it again.

But soon after the post, I received a direct message from someone on Instagram. They were saying that I should not "overdo" Christian talk because it might turn some of my followers off. I read the message and took it in my stride: on social media people are quick to say what they want to whoever and however they want to. There are no boundaries, and I let it go.

A little later, the conversation started to bother me and I thought, "No, I can't let this slide." I mean, it was borderline bullying: How can this person tell me what to do on my own page? As far as I was concerned, because God is part of my life, anyone on my social media pages will come across Scripture and church-related things.

I decided get it off my chest by talking to my brother Ntlafatso about it, but I was still not taking it too seriously. I told him, "Can you believe what they are saying to me on my own page?"

More time passed and the issue persisted, and by then I had posted to my Instagram story saying, "On this page, you will hear about God. It will be 'Jesus this, Jesus that'. If you don't like that, you can unfollow."

In the days that followed, I began to see people talking online about "Jesus this, Jesus that", taking on the phrase as a label, adding it to their bios, and choosing variations of it for their usernames. Now it was becoming something! My brother had the idea to print the slogan on T-shirts and sell them. He funded the printing and we were ready to sell the T-shirts, but then the Holy Spirit interrupted and said, "No, that's not what this is."

I felt guided to go to Joburg Theatre and ask them when their next opening was. They told us that in three weeks we could have a space that seats 250 people. We booked it, with no idea what would happen next. In those three weeks, God's voice became louder and I saw His hand over this new, unknown project. God brought people to volunteer with lighting and sound, people offering to perform … it was all coming together. We had the first event in March 2023 where people came, paid no admission fee because that's what God had said, and gathered to share the Word, pray and worship.

And we've just been carrying on with that work at every new opportunity that God gives us. *Jesus This, Jesus That* has allowed me to tune into community in a way I haven't done in a while. It's not about me preaching or leading or otherwise making myself the figurehead of some movement. It's about getting to know more people whose hearts are on fire for God, and opening myself up to witness what can happen when believers work together towards a common goal. I am grateful to be working alongside all those who give their time, energy and resources for the cause.

What this project has taught me, and continues to show me, is to trust God, follow His voice and follow through on His instructions even – and especially – when it makes no sense. Each time we organise another event, I ask, "What next, Lord? How do we do this?" – and He answers. The work has become a consistent practice of intentionally and deliberately pursuing God.

Jesus This, Jesus That came to me at a time when I was struggling with my faith. I was experiencing deep grief and at that moment God brought me a new, ever-expanding way to strengthen my relationship with Him – the core of that is doing what He has instructed believers to do: go out and fetch others, and bring them to Him.

As I have gotten older and been part of faith communities outside of my home, I have struggled with the concept of "church". Attending some church services feels like a big production. It felt forced – not at all like the family and community that I grew up with. Some of the churches I have seen today are cold, and people seem so detached from one another.

Take the example of how people show up for each other in the event of a funeral. Everyone is right there at the house, welcoming guests, chopping vegetables to prepare meals. As black people, we don't just send flowers when there's a death in someone's family. We were raised to gather and show full support in other people's lives. Church was so intertwined in our daily living. Now it feels like a separate area, with none of the same safety and warmth.

I struggle with church now. It feels like a very disconnected place and I have had to learn how to be discerning when looking for a faith community.

Moving from home to a new city, as I did when I started at the University of Pretoria, comes with a feeling of displacement, and half the struggle of settling down is finding places that feel familiar, where you can belong. In my case, moving from Bloemfontein to Pretoria and later Johannesburg meant finding a church that matched my upbringing.

When we were growing up, my mother allowed us to explore a variety of churches, but always with the theme of discipline and truth. So, while we were reciting verses from memory at one church, we were learning new hymns at a Baptist church with a mostly white congregation, which added an extra element of how people from different cultures worship – and then we were taking on even more different styles of teaching and learning the Word when we went on mission trips.

That is why church, for me, has never been one thing or looked one way. Sure, I had a home base at Christian Revival Church (CRC), even finding a branch of the church while I was at university, but from there I always felt free to go where I felt called.

Under my mother's watchful eye, I learned that church was a place where Jesus was at the centre, where the Word of God was preached in an undiluted way, where I would be encouraged to read the Word and pray. If these things – which I would say are the basis of salvation – were there, I felt comfortable.

Importantly, I look for my church to be a place where I can find guidance for navigating life's issues when they arise. Church is serious to me because it's where I go to strengthen my faith and receive encouragement to keep on living my faith out loud.

One obstacle I have experienced is being recognised as a "famous somebody" in church. What I want from church is to feel at home, and to be in fellowship with other believers. I have struggled finding a church where I am able to be myself; there have been times when people try to make me part of the leadership structure within weeks of knowing me. Where is the discipleship in that?

The church, as far as it relates to different faith groups and their worship structures, makes it incredibly difficult for people who are popular or well known or rich to be ordinary worshippers because as soon as they step through the doors, they are seen only for what they do for a living.

In my experience, people change their attitude toward me as soon as they recognise me. They see "Rorisang Thandekiso, MC and television personality" – not me, as a person.

Why can't I go to a church and sit at the back? Why do people immediately want to find me a "special" seat? Why do people feel that they can come up to me during a vulnerable moment of worship to talk about something they saw on TV or in the papers?

Ke tlile kerekeng. Why can't I come to church and lift up my hands without feeling ten pairs of curious eyes on me? Trying to see how I pray and asking me, "so wa mo rata Ntate Modimo, ne?"

It was as if they hadn't expected my love for God to be so evident, so undeniable. Always this question: "Is she for real?"

It's just that it's on social media now – but I have never not been this. I've been preaching and praising all my life. I think it was Dr Rebecca Malope who once said that sometimes all we want to do is go to church and cry – but once you are in the public eye, that becomes very difficult to do.

People looking for what they think is this great example of a faith-led life are only seeing what I put on social media and making their own sometimes misguided interpretations of it. Some people see me praying or preaching the message and incorporate it into their lives as they see best. Others fixate on the fact that the message is coming through me – someone who they see as "exceptional" – and speak not about what I am teaching but about me. They lose sight of the message and are blinded by celebrity.

I have found that what saves me from the chaos is the fact that I chose, a long time ago, to fall in love with the Word of God for myself. The foundation is within me, and doesn't rely on any external church. Seeing God in my life for myself, seeing what He has done for me, how He has guided me, being in constant conversation with Him – that's what gives me security in my faith.

I really do appreciate my earlier days. If I hadn't had the radical Jesus upbringing that I had, I don't think that I would be able to be who I am. It solidified something in me that I saw many of my colleagues struggling with as we were coming up in the entertainment industry: the idea that you are *enough*.

Our industry perpetuates the idea of "we've got to add on to you ..." Hair, make-up, lashes, expensive clothes, cars … It never stops. I am grateful for my strong faith foundation, which helps me to overcome the doubts and obstacles that the industry puts in my way.

I've got permission to be myself in all ways because God has affirmed in me that I am enough.

Working to survive

My first job was when I was 15. I was a waitress at Maxi's (a well-known coffee shop), working on Fridays after school, doing a double shift on Saturdays and then on Sunday mornings before church. This was the year after the fire. Money was extremely tight as my family was starting from scratch. We were renting part of my mom's friend's house, and so it was important that I worked.

At school, the Life Orientation teacher introduced us to the "work certificate", which we could apply for so that we could find jobs as part of the requirements of the curriculum. That certificate became my "in", an easy way to get a job without having to explain why I, as a child, needed to work. I received my certificate, went for an interview and got my first waitressing job.

Because Maxi's was in the middle of a shopping mall, I was in a position to see what everyone in town was doing, especially over the weekend. On Fridays, I would see people from school milling about; when the movies ended, they would come down the escalators, which were right by the restaurant, and I would see my school-mates. I could feel their excitement, especially at month-end when spirits were high because pocket money was in. And I would be there, working.

My time as a waitress introduced me to people from all walks of life. At work, to a certain extent, we're all on the same level; we work for one boss, we have the same duties. It's different from school or other environments. Knowing this, I saw that the world was indeed a strange place. How else could I explain wiping tables and carrying food alongside people with professional degrees?

That's when I became aware of the issues immigrants faced: at the time, teachers and various other professionals were moving to South Africa in their numbers, many of them from Zimbabwe, hoping for better employment prospects. I remember I had a colleague, Mr Moyo, who was a qualified Mathematics teacher. We worked together at Gold Rush Grillhouse in 2005. I suppose we had that small thing in common: we were working to make things better for our families.

I built strong relationships with my co-workers and, because I was the youngest, I did find a kind of "parental" connection with them. The chef at Gold Rush, who we all called Tata, took me under his wing and made sure my working days ran as smoothly as possible.

It was clear that he was looking after me, making sure I was properly fed. We had a staff meal at lunch, but on the days when this meal comprised something I couldn't eat, such as liver and pap, Tata would prepare something on the side for me. He would use some of the salvageable leftovers, fixing the food into something nice just for me.

I felt special when he made what came to be my favourite snack: fried and spiced potato peels. His care extended to my career in food service, as it was. He would teach me about food preparation and about how the restaurant worked.

He's the one who taught me what "medium rare" looked like. He'd coach me on the dishes on the menu, making me recite ingredients so that I would be able to repeat them properly for the customers at my tables.

By the time I wrote the test to become a permanent staff member, I was cruising. I didn't hesitate on any of the questions that could've tripped me up because Tata had spent time teaching me. He saved me from mistakes and encouraged me to play to my strengths. He said I should use what I have: to tell the people that I was still in school and not to downplay the fact, and also not to downplay the fact that I can speak Afrikaans.

With his guidance, I became a much better waiter and even had some regulars. In time, I had customers so invested in me that they would pay for me to go to debating tournaments! It was all thanks to Tata.

Days were long and difficult, but none as long as that Sunday in 2005 when a customer died at a restaurant table.

He was there with his wife and child, and he ordered a Black Label draught. I took the drink and their food to the table, and noticed that the man was looking a little uncomfortable. A short while later he asked for a second beer and his wife asked for a glass of water. When I came back from the bar, I saw the man's body suddenly go limp as he slid off the chair onto the ground. I immediately called out for a doctor, hoping to get help. While I was standing close to him thinking of what to do next, one of the customers from a nearby table let me know that she believed he was dead. She said it quietly, so as not to further alarm the family.

It was the middle of a service delivery strike, and because of that, emergency service providers had basically halted all transport vehicles, so getting police, doctors or ambulances to any scene was impossible.

I had to run out of the shopping centre and over the street to ask for help from the nearest doctors' rooms. I ran in, told the receptionist that my customer was dying, and asked for someone to come back to the restaurant with me.

The doctor drove to the restaurant and I ran back after him. (Of course, because I was black and he was white, he was not going to let me ride in his car.) When I caught up with him, he confirmed that my customer was indeed dead. I knew that people had been trying to revive him, giving him CPR, pumping away at his chest, but it had been in vain.

We moved the man's body from the back of the restaurant to the front, and covered him in tablecloths. And I had to carry on with my shift. Sunday is a very busy day on the restaurant floor and business was not going to stop for a dead man.

It must have been over four hours before anyone came to fetch the man's body. In that time, I was aware that his family was in their car, shaken, waiting. It was a harsh reality that no one could shield me from: I was not a teenager in that moment, I was a waitress with obligations to her manager. I blocked it out as best I could and I pushed through the rest of my shift with no help from the other staffers. It was the longest day of my 16-year-old life.

While people were closing up their orders and asking for takeaways because they'd realised there was a dead body in the restaurant, the kitchen was still operating and my boss was carrying on as if everything was normal. When the police arrived, I was the one responsible for telling them what had happened, reliving the events of that strange afternoon.

A few weeks later, the man's wife came back to the restaurant to thank me.

My mother was very worried when she heard what had happened. She couldn't believe that her child had had to experience something so traumatic.

I continued to work at Gold Rush until my matric year. After some time, the signage showed wear and the "L" in "Gold" fell off. We staff members started to joke that the name "God Rush" was fitting, because it seemed that's where people came to make their final stop before leaving earth.

Work was a natural complement to my burgeoning debating career. I entered competitions with the aim of winning and taking home the all-important prize money. The two, three or even six thousand rand that I would win meant a dramatic improvement in my family's immediate circumstances, even after I handed part of my winnings over to my school.

At the time, my mother's financial situation didn't allow her to comfortably pay our school fees, so any little bit helped. And then a big competition with a R12 000 prize came up, and I immediately thought, "Won't that close the debt?"

During my matric year, I was named the Young Communicator of the Year. In 2008, I was chosen to represent the country in the Global Young Leaders Summit that was held in America, where I was ranked third out of 400 representatives from across the world.

I was doing well at debating and my school supported me all the way. When an international speaking competition took place – the Young Communicator of the Year Award – the Department of Education brought buses of people from the Vaal to support me. I was the pride of the school and the district, which was wonderful, but part of me did think, "Why would they bring all these people? What if I get to America and flunk the competition?!"

But my reputation preceded me and companies were excited to sponsor me. I remember talking to Ntate Jeff Radebe (a minister at the time) about what I needed ahead of the trip, and taking that as an opportunity to express my desire for funding for a university education. All the money they were spending to sponsor my trip? That could easily be my university fees! People from a number of local transport agencies were instructed to help me with what I needed to make that dream come true.

I left South Africa with a new laptop and the promise of studying further after high school!

And that was what debating was to me: an opportunity to make life better, a way out. In taking on competitions and finding work as a waitress, my objective was clear: I wanted to lighten my mother's load. That's all I had in mind.

All my tips were dedicated to making things easier for my mom and my siblings: money for bread and milk, money for transport. It meant treats for the house now and then; eventually I was also able to pay for a DStv subscription for the family.

I got to a point where I was self-sufficient enough to pay for my own school outings. I would tell my mom, "School is hosting this event" and the date, but when she asked me how much I needed, I'd say, "Don't worry, it's sorted". I was in a position to not only pay for myself but also for my best friend Eva, who was like family to me.

Winning competitions and working part-time meant that I could help take care of my family. They didn't need to worry about household needs or about the car that needed fixing. I was even able to pay for my own matric dance dress. At every step, I took on the responsibility of closing the financial gap.

Years later, at my thirtieth birthday party, my mother stood up to give a speech and revealed something that I hadn't been aware of. At the time when I was taking on extra shifts at restaurants and working late, giving over most of my earnings so that the family could live more comfortably, my focus had been on making things easier for my mom. I had not considered the personal cost to her.

At that birthday celebration, my mother shared how she'd been so anxious, staying up late at night waiting for my shifts to end so that she could fetch me. She'd agonise about how our family situation had pushed her young child to go out and work. It was difficult for her to make peace with her daughter working so hard.

It was revelatory because I had been so singular in my focus, thinking only of making things better. My thought was, "But I was doing it for you", whereas my mother was thinking about how a child should not have been in that situation.

What's important is that I was able to find those opportunities to positively contribute to my family's life. The personal cost is as good as written off because the rewards God has shown me for the work that I put in during that time are beyond measure.

It's amazing that public speaking took me so far because in my early school years I was constantly told that I was "too talkative". Teachers sent the message that being expressive was a bad thing. In Grade 7, I excelled academically but I was not chosen as a prefect, all because of my reputation of talking too much, being "tjatjarag". My issue was that I challenged the teachers too much. Not being chosen while my best friend Eva was, crushed me. I did eventually get over it, but it certainly affected my self-esteem.

Still, my voice was the strongest thing about me. My teachers could also see that, and I remember those who encouraged me.

My primary-school English teacher, Miss Sermon, was one of the first to focus on the gift in me. In class, we often had to prepare speeches for marks. Each student would get up in front of the class and deliver a speech. To manage the process, teachers called on us in alphabetical order. I knew that my group, "T", would usually only make our speeches on the second day, so on the first day I waited. As each of my classmates made their presentation, I would listen and critique, asking myself, "How can I make this better?"

Sometimes, when it was my turn, I would challenge myself to see if I could get 10 out of 10 by freestyling. Miss Sermon knew this but she didn't count it against me. (But when she noticed that it was all in my head, she made a general class rule that we would all have to show her where our speeches were written down.)

One of my most memorable speeches, and the one that really got Miss Sermon's attention, featured a Kirk Franklin song. At the time, Kirk Franklin was known for music that highlighted social justice issues and called on people to step up, all with a clear Christian message. I took one of these songs – I remember it used the sound of a heart beating – and used it as the foundation of my speech. I played the first part of the song until it got to the sound of a hospital monitor beeping. At that "flat-lining" sound, I started my speech.

Miss Sermon saw that there was so much behind my love for asking questions and my excellent comprehension skills. She introduced me to the idea of going to study at the National School of the Arts; she got the forms and was ready to vouch for me. I was excited about the idea and took it to my mom. Unfortunately, boarding schools had a terrible reputation at the time and my mother didn't want me to go to a school where "all the children did drugs".

In a continued show of faith, Miss Sermon asked me to write that year's Grade 7 valedictory speech. But I was still not a prefect, so I wouldn't be delivering it; my friend Eva would. I remember coaching Eva through the speech at break. She was my closest friend and I was happy for her success, but at the same time I started to think that there was something about me that just wouldn't get me "chosen" for these accolades; my perception of "success" was changing. A part of me felt not good enough.

After Grade 4, when I had to repeat my year, my confidence had been tempered: I was still outgoing and outspoken, because that's my God-given personality, but I don't think I was thriving. Yet it's undeniable that Grade 7 was my best academic year. Perhaps that early drive to succeed was coming from a subconscious knowledge that the high-school years ahead would be incredibly demanding.

At the beginning of high school, I met a teacher who would continue the work that Miss Sermon started with me. Mr Muhaddin was an old, shortish Indian man with glasses; he was my Grade 8 English teacher. One day he asked me, "Do you like writing?" I was reluctant to say yes but I told him, "I love formulating in my mind". He said that's writing – "You're just lazy!" Mr Muhaddin believed in me and knew I had the potential to do well in writing and speaking. That's why he didn't hesitate to enter me in the English Olympiad even though it was only open to Grade 11s and 12s. He managed to push my entry through; I competed and I won! But this was also an early obstacle in my public speaking career: I won, but I did not get the prize because of my age.

Nevertheless, the seed was planted: I realised I could make real money through public speaking. Each competition I entered after that, I won. With money on my mind, I had no other option but to beat the competitors.

I came from a home where my mother had financial issues and my siblings and I only knew second-hand clothing. My mother took great care of our clothes and taught us to value what we found at thrift stores. We never felt like we were missing out on anything – but we were aware that we had less than other children had.

The other learners at these competitions had no idea how hungry I was to win. My mindset was just so completely different. Debating separated me from the group; it created a name for me. Eva, Musa (Mthombeni) and I were a fantastic team; with them by my side I stepped into my power as first speaker. I began to feel that I'd found where I belonged.

At around the time when I was hitting my stride with debating, things at home were also shaking up. My mother was under pressure and it started to manifest in illness. In response, I ramped things up with debating and public speaking, so I could earn money to help my mom. Winning or losing is the difference between paying school fees or having to stay home. In the following years, when I was debating and travelling and studying and working, I was under a great deal of strain.

I couldn't find a way to express that and, thinking about it now, I can say for sure that my high-school years were *exhausting*.

Making the rands make sense

From when I was young, money as a problem solver was foremost in my mind. It was a solution to daily concerns and a way to make the immediate future a little more comfortable for my people. I didn't view it as a way to freedom, per se. I didn't use up my money just because I had it, or spend large amounts at a time just for myself. I grew up watching my mother work hard to earn the money she needed for us, sometimes borrowing to make ends meet, and I learned how much of a precious resource it was. I was determined to learn how to make money work for me.

At university, when I was in a routine doing TV work, I started sending money home. That was my priority, alongside sustaining myself in the city.

Later, after I had graduated and once I'd kept my media jobs for a few years, earning steadily, I decided to put aside some time and money for myself. For my twenty-seventh birthday I took myself to Plettenberg Bay and went bungee jumping; I decided to make it an annual tradition to treat myself to a solo trip, to carve out time to truly rest.

I started exploring the idea that it was okay for me to use the money I work so hard to earn on making myself happy. I could do the right thing with financial planning, help my mother out – and still do my hair, if I wanted to, or something as simple as buying myself an ice cream.

In a way, being super careful with money and starting to work early in life contributed to me becoming resourceful and unique when it came to personal style. On YoTV, we didn't have stylists or a wardrobe department, so I had to find ways to keep myself looking "cool" on a budget. That's when I started leaning into thrifting and developing a taste for fun, affordable fashion. (This was, of course, blossoming from a seed my mother had planted years before, when she first taught us to take pride in everything we put on, no matter where it came from.)

I didn't feel the need to keep up with new clothes, cars and the like, as most young people do when they start earning money. The validation that is often attached to that kind of conspicuous consumption, I'd already received from my mother. We were raised to feel like were enough, and that helped us in making wise life decisions about our future.

I had priorities and I let those dictate my budget and spending. This discipline was so important to me, and enjoyment and pleasure were so far removed from my conception of money that when I was about 19 years old, I remember feeling guilty for weeks after spending my first tax-return monies. For the first time since I'd started working, I had a lump sum of money, but after it was gone, I realised that I needed to respect money and spend it with discipline and intention. If I take care of my money, it will take care of me.

Internal discipline met external advice and divine timing, and I was able to purchase my first property at 23 years old.

I had been renting for some time, saving money while I shared the rent on a house in Parkhurst with two other young women. All along I was thinking, "What's the next best move to make? I know I'm not going to rent forever".

When I was ready to take that next step, and after going to the bank to enquire about a home loan, I went to open houses, looking for my first house. At one of these showings, I met an older white woman, an estate agent, who generously explained to me that the loan the bank had approved me for was not the best decision I could make. I showed the estate agent my pre-approval and she said, "No". Then for about 30 to 45 minutes, this woman, who I had not known until that afternoon, sat down with me and gave me a crash course in financial literacy for young adults. She explained that firstly I should keep my credit card debt low; then I should apply to purchase a house at a lower price than the bank would have tied me to, and that I should pay a percentage more on the bond each month so that the interest rate could decrease over time. She opened my eyes, and that conversation with her has helped me with my financial decisions ever since. It was honestly the best advice ever.

The way I take responsibility for my money is also tied to my childhood, to a fear of going back to a difficult situation. I can't go back there, and I think about that all the time. But the stakes are always high: as a freelancer I'm constantly thinking about tomorrow. When I was younger and started appearing on TV, I didn't fit the glamorous child star narrative; for myself and some of my colleagues who came from a similar home situation, we were working children and had a responsibility to a household back home.

Working from a young age and having to keep up with school and debating, and also making sure everyone at home was okay, was incredibly difficult. However, I don't feel regret. Instead, I feel grateful for the experience because it helped shape me into someone who knows how to keep multiple projects going and do well in all of them. That period in my life moulded me into who I am.

We inherit our money habits from our parents. The anxiety around not having enough, the focus on having enough to meet obligations, the worry about spending too much on "unnecessary" things. Those things do still come up for me. And yet I don't think of my responsibilities to my family as "black tax". That was a term I often heard when I began working. People would grumble about how they had to give their parents money and couldn't "enjoy" their salaries. I could not relate.

The Bible says in 1 Timothy 5:8, "Anyone who does not provide for their relatives, and especially for their own household, has denied the faith and is worse than an unbeliever." It says we must take care of our people, of our immediate family.

I see it as my duty to help provide for my family and I am grateful that God gives me the opportunities to work, to earn money. And I will gladly use my resources to open up my mother's world. Before the Covid-19 pandemic slowed down international travel, I had worked enough to be in a position to send my mom overseas several times. She has been to Europe and to Asia, and each time I have dropped her off at the airport, I have been excited to hear her talk about travelling to places even I haven't seen. Those conversations are precious because I could never have imagined being able to give these experiences to her. Given how we grew up, this was not how her story is "supposed" to end.

I look also at my grandmother, who used to gather up her grandkids for day trips around Bloemfontein, taking us to the museum or to the botanical gardens in an effort to expand our little worlds. She wanted to show us how much more there is out there. Now, I gladly return the favour.

The reason I so freely give these experiences back to the women who raised me is because they showed me that kindness first, they gave me that gift first.

To do God's work, you must move

In 2008, I won *Seventeen* magazine's Next Big Thing competition, in the Arts category. Before I could really process what was happening, I was flying to Cape Town for the photoshoot. In a phone call with the team from the magazine, they asked me to say something about my win. I still wonder where my head was at that moment. I said: "Everybody in my category needs something external to express themselves. I don't even need a mic. It just comes out of me. My gift is to communicate, and I can do it anytime, anywhere, under any circumstances. I can be who I am, always."

That was my winning speech.

Looking back, I think it was bound to happen: at Young Communicators in that same year (2008), I was voted Most Likely to be the Next Big Thing; and years later when I started at YoTV, there were some people who said, "We knew it!"

YoTV and *Blue Couch* happened in the least expected way. I didn't audition, but I was called in for a screen test. It turned out that Musa (Mthombeni, my schoolmate and friend, who had begun working on YoTV at that time) was around when the executives saw a clip of one of my speeches at Young Communicators. They were impressed with what they saw, got my details from Musa, and I was called in for the test. Two weeks later, I was live on air as the presenter of *Blue Couch*, a youth-centred current-affairs talk show.

I hadn't considered pursuing a career in TV. It may have been Musa's thing, but I never thought of it as mine. Still, I feel that the transition from a strong academic performance to debating to television happened organically. This was 2009, my first year of varsity, and I was pursuing a degree in international relations – it was a continuation of my school-long interest in justice, the next best expression of it.

I was doing Model United Nations, signing up for all the student societies that aligned with my interests. But in the end, I found that the best way to connect with people on important issues was through *Blue Couch*. As scary as it was in the first couple of episodes, I found my footing. The topics on the show related perfectly with what I was studying. It was what I had always loved to do: talking to people, bringing a point across. It was what I had done as first speaker. My opening link on *Blue Couch* felt a lot like the opening statements I would make at debating tournaments. That's why it felt natural to me. I thought, "I've done this!"

And then *Blue Couch* just ... blew. At one point it felt like I was "Oprah for the kids"!

Soon, I was producing my own episodes. One day I complained that the show's planned episode was boring. The commissioning editor, Lolly Gibson, heard me and challenged me on this. She told me to research and pitch some ideas. From then on, I had to put a script together every two weeks. I learned how to put a show together. But I was in – no turning back.

I only had one job that wasn't in media, and that was at Winning Teams. On the recommendation from Akhumzi Jezile (may his soul rest in peace), who was part of the YoTV ecosystem and had become a friend, I started work as a facilitator on an education programme that focused on rural areas.

With my colleague, I would be on the road to remote areas of the country, connecting with teachers and sharing a Maths, Science and Engineering-focused boardgame with them. The game, *Winning Teams*, was used to teach educators how to make the subjects more accessible to learners. There I was, fresh in my twenties, travelling the country and working with rural communities. In a way, the earlier years of mission trips with the church had prepared me for this.

Working at Winning Teams opened my eyes to the world. During that year, I learned that there was more to the world than Johannesburg. After working so closely with these communities, I also had a renewed perspective of who my *Blue Couch* audience was, who my show had to engage with.

After I left YoTV, I had the opportunity to work on DStv for *One Gospel* and *Dumisa*. This is where I became strong as a producer; I was in front of the camera for two shows, and I was producing those and one other. Producing was my nine-to-five and took me deeper into South Africa as well as across the continent. I was having to stretch myself in order to reach and engage with people in different segments.

The majority of my colleagues were Nigerian and I was gaining popularity with the West African audience. Soon I was given the nickname Chiomaka, and I even used it as part of my daily opening link at *Good Morning Africa*, opening new episodes with, "Good morning to you, my name is Rori, known across Africa as Chiomaka, and you're tuned into *Good Morning Africa*, the biggest and brightest breakfast show …"

Taking everything together – debating in school, the missionary work, the time in the RCL, my first jobs as a waitress – I see that life had prepared me for this next chapter at DStv. I was equipped with skills to deal with an audience, connect with people, build networks. I knew how to direct a project and get the best out of a team, and how to give credit where it's due.

My life experience crafted my presenting style: when I'm in front of the camera, I value getting close to the people, relating on some level. I'm the girl next door who you can talk to about anything. My career and work style are the way that they are because of how I've lived. And that is important to me, because a part of me still feels like that little girl who was looking at every opportunity as the next break: through my work, I feel the need to continue to be there for her.

Always at the back of my mind I'm thinking, am I doing well? Am I honouring God? Am I making my family proud?

I don't think of my career trajectory in "moments". I don't think, "Yes, *that* was a Big Moment". Each new challenge, each new job feels like a big break. Every chance is big; the stakes are always high. The only option is to go forward.

There are also the added financial and societal factors: as much as we in the Arts don't want to admit it, we are always trying to prove to family, to parents, that we made the right choice. It's like, "All the 'normal' things that you wish for me, I'm going to be able to do – and sometimes even better."

Things have happened in such a way that I haven't kept a CV and I hardly go for traditional interviews. I have contract meetings with people who are interested in building valuable working relationships. And, because I'm constantly thinking about what to do next, where the next opportunity is, I'm the kind of person who looks at each new contract and thinks: what can I get out of this? That's not just about money: it's about how I can make the most of the job, how I can benefit from it.

For example, when I was on *Good Morning Africa*: I knew that the job was not about the money. I was getting paid very little, in fact. However, the job literally opened up a new world for me. I was able to travel all over the continent, seeing things and places that I wouldn't be able to afford on my own. The benefit was not monetary, it was experiential. And it was an experience that changed my life and gave me skills that could take me further in my career.

While working at *Good Morning Africa* with Wale, my producer, I learned how to leverage connections to create content. We had travelled together to Lagos in Nigeria for an assignment, and at an early point in our trip, Wale had business to attend to in another part of the country. He left me alone in Lagos for two weeks with the instruction to "create content" – I had to come up with material for several episodes of television, on the spot.

That's how *This is My House* was born: a lifestyle show that featured popular celebrities at home in their city. Thanks to the relationships I had previously built with their managers, I was able to secure screen time with the likes of D'banj, Davido and even Tiwa Savage, who we flagged down for an interview in the middle of a grocery store. There may even have been a private jet involved in one of our episodes … It was quite an adventure.

What Wale had done was throw me right into the deep end and wait for me to sink or swim. And I swam. Wale's assignment confirmed for me that I was a content producer – and I could do it anywhere in the world.

I was the youngest on the team and I had just proven that I had the tenacity to make great television, to find the stories and do the work. After that trip, I headed up the channel's Nigerian office as the executive producer.

Through that job, I saw the world, built strong industry connections and, perhaps best of all, learned to get over the fear of doing big, new things.

When I worked at *One Gospel*, I was honing my production skills but I also had a bigger goal in mind: with a contract like that, I could establish myself as a "stable" person in the eyes of the banks. As we know, freelancers struggle to get support from financial institutions for loans or credit; we are seen as a liability. With the *One Gospel* contract, I could be taken seriously. Through that job I was able to afford and secure my first car and property. It was about more than just the job; it was about my future security.

As my career grew from strength to strength, I focused not on the money – though, of course, it was essential for my and my family's quality of life – but on the relationships. The main question was: How long can I maintain a relationship with this business or client, and what can it lead to?

By learning where I fitted in and who I best worked with, I became more confident in my abilities and started to see my worth in the industry. This was my field, and I was becoming better and better; my work started to mean more. I realised that it didn't matter where I worked or who released the payments, because I was valuable.

The concept of myself as a versatile content creator who can connect deeply with the audience explains why I prefer not to "claim" any company, client, production house, agency, etc. I can't be sold to the highest bidder in that way; instead, I pursue and welcome opportunities based on how much my craft – broadcasting and storytelling – will be valued there.

I don't put names of radio stations in my bio; I don't

post brands on my Instagram. I don't present myself as an ambassador or even as a staff member anywhere. I focus on doing what I'm good at.

My niche is down-home, humble, friendly and relatable – glitz and glam is not for me. I am not a "performer" in that way. I know that my current job sets me up for my next one: as a freelancer, you're only as good as your last gig.

I don't see my life in "moments", but I am aware that some jobs or projects pushed me in a direction that changed things forever. I can point to Lesedi FM as the gig that awakened a new part of my public persona, allowing me to be even more authentic in my work. Lesedi FM is a respected Sesotho radio station with a focus on keeping language and culture thriving. Getting behind the mic was like a homecoming: I took my history and my family along with me to my shifts. The show was for all of us. It was like the return of the prodigal daughter: our Sotho star who has gone all over the world with her talent is coming home to share her gift with us, in our language.

It really stretched me. Because I hadn't been living at home for so long – I'd been in Joburg, working, living and thinking mostly in English – I knew that the Sotho I spoke was no longer the genuine article: non-speakers would hear me and think nothing of it, but my mother could tell that something in the tone and vocabulary had changed. By the time the Lesedi FM job came along, I had already decided to make an effort to relearn the language, to get my Sesotho back.

The challenge was about regaining competence and confidence in my home language. Could I *connect* in Sesotho? Could I hold a show? Be witty? These are the questions that made my time at Lesedi FM rich and fulfilling. I am proud of the work I did there. I experienced real growth and came away with a reaffirmed love for my people.

I would say it's this love of people that underpins my other life-changing project, *Jesus This, Jesus That.*

When it took off, I thought, "Maybe this is what turns people's hearts away from me" – I thought it would lose me support. I didn't expect much from it. Instead, it has become an amplifier for my other work, and it's taking me places I've never been before. With the positive reception it received, and people's eagerness to participate and to help it grow and to spread the Word in this unexpected way, I can't deny that this is a shift in my career. I can't downplay it.

It's all new to me: I've never before had security guards at the airport stopping me to say, "You're the girl with the verses, on Tik Tok!" I'm trying to figure it out, trying to see what it can do next – but that's when the Holy Spirit reminds me who's really in charge.

With *Jesus This, Jesus That*, I feel my career and faith are one in a way that they haven't been before.

I have always had this drive to succeed and I can point to my teen years as the space where it was first cultivated. I had to push myself forward and make a plan all through school – I didn't know any other way.

I thank God that I was saved at that time because the struggle of my teen years was immense. It's only through the grace of God that mentally and spiritually I was able to get through it. There were so many things that could have easily derailed me, made me feel less than, convinced me that I shouldn't go for the things I wanted to go for.

If my mind was not fixated on doing the right thing – serving God, being conscious of my faith – I would have made different decisions. It was a very traumatic time. There was so much happening at school and at home that I don't know how I came out of it. My only answer is through Jesus.

One thing that was evident was that God had a way of reassuring me. Throughout every season, God had my back. Winning competitions, being chosen for travel opportunities, finding favour at work …

I've always known I was special, but not in a cocky way. God just has my back.

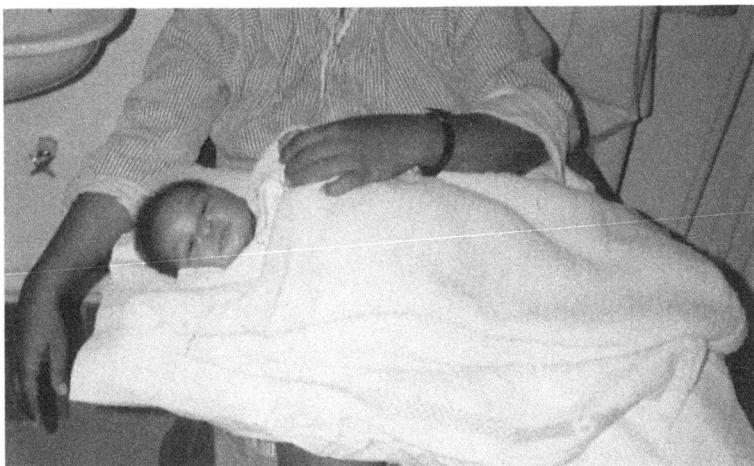
I was born on the 9 August 1989 in
Pelonomi Hospital Bloemfontein.

My first birthday with my first car and my first church dress.
Spot the red boots!

Turning three years old and already a lively and bubbly child,
I wore the same pink church dress wore at my first birthday.

With Bokang, my elder sister and my first friend.
She remains by my side even today.

With my little brother Ntlafatso, the baby of the family. My best friend.

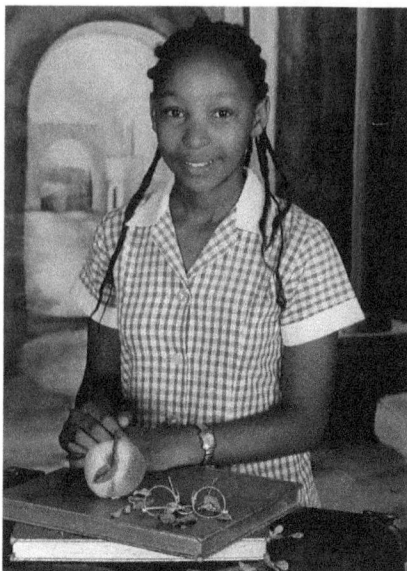
Photo day at Milton Primary, Grade 7.

Riverside High school junior dance.
Ponytail braids were a way of life! Lol!

Grade 9, Riverside High school portraits.

Me and mom at a family wedding, best friends.

Photoshoot for this book cover in 2024.

Photoshoot for this book cover in 2024.

Photoshoot for this book cover in 2024.

The family that made me

As the middle child, I have a special vantage point in my family. I am close enough to my mother to know the rules and discipline, and I am close enough to my siblings to have created my own personality and made a claim on the world in ways that earn me their respect. I am a child with a big view of the world – and the curiosity I was born with helps me explore both spaces and meld them into one.

For most of my early years, I saw the world through the eyes of my older sister, Bokang. She was my first example of everything: how to behave, what to wear, how to move in the world. She was the north on my compass. Bokang and I were best friends for my formative years. I looked up to her.

As the first grandchild in the family, Bokang was the apple of my grandfather's eye. Between Bokang and myself, he had his hands full: he would take us to school, drop us back home, and generally dote on us at every opportunity.

My grandfather loved us through his time and through his actions. And, like any grandfather worth his salt, he spoiled us. I remember how, having realised that I shared his and my mother's affinity for animals, my grandfather brought me a puppy. He drove all the way from Bloemfontein to the Vaal to give me Princess.

Not content with giving me presents to make me happy, my elders were also intentional about letting me be the outspoken, curious child that I was. They didn't make me lower my voice or dim my light; instead, they watched as I explored the world, supporting me. After all, is there much anyone can do when their toddler bounces over to a stranger's dog and puts her hand in its mouth? When I think of that story, it confirms for me that I have always been a free-spirited, open-hearted person who's ready to learn.

My older sister, who was learning about the world two years before I was born, has a more considered, quieter approach to life. As the firstborn, there is, of course, a more serious air of duty and discipline around her. She's the strict intellectual of the family and her no-nonsense attitude meant that her relationship with me seesawed between sister and "deputy mom" a lot of the time.

I wanted to be wherever she was, doing whatever she was doing. We wore exactly the same outfits with exactly the same hairstyle for the first few years of our lives together. I enjoyed it because it allowed me to relate to this fascinating older sibling of mine.

People would think we were twins, and I loved having my very own best friend.

As we got older and Bokang reached that crucial age of 13 before me, she started to create her own identity. Clothes went from identical, to only matching in colour, to not being similar at all. My sister was pulling away from me, and that hurt. (Two or three years later, it was my turn to reach teendom, and I understood exactly how she'd been feeling.)

Before all that, though, a third sibling joined us: my brother Ntlafatso.

My sister and I, having spent the last eight years with only each other in our world, were very excited for this new friend.

My brother was a light that everyone turned towards in the family; the baby, who took up all our time and attention. It meant that I was no longer the youngest one who was doted over, but it also gave me a new sibling to care for.

Whereas I had looked up to Bokang for guidance, I started to look to Ntlafatso as my responsibility. I knew even then that I had a talent for looking after children, and I tapped into that with my brother, showing him how to navigate the world of our family. I was now the Big Sister, and I took that title seriously.

My brother's arrival would later soothe the transition between me and Bokang: while she grew up and separated herself from us young ones, I could take any feelings of rejection and channel them into my relationship with Ntlafatso. When Bokang would choose to read a book instead of playing, or start to say that no one was allowed in her room, I would go to my new friend and we would make our own fun.

I was so invested in Ntlafatso that I would complain whenever he had to stay home while we went to town. Travelling anywhere with babies can be tedious, and to show this my mother would say that whoever brought my brother along had to take responsibility for carrying him around. Now, he may have been the baby of the family but he was also a big boy: imagine carrying around a baby who already weighed 5 kilograms at birth? But that was me: I carried my brother through the shops and, when I needed a break, I would find somewhere to put him down. Sometimes that would mean leaving him on a patch of carpet inside Edgars!

Those days started our lifelong closeness, and made us partners in life. And if we were partners, then Bokang was our leader. She encouraged us, in her own way, to stand on our own two feet. When it came to school,

Bokang did not give me the easy way out. I remember how I used to ask her for help with English homework and, instead of giving me the answers, she would push me to do my own research. I would ask something like, "What does 'prodigy' mean?" and Bokang would say, "Spell it", and then hand me a dictionary so I could look it up.

She was always there to help us navigate the world. In true big-sister fashion, she made executive decisions that were for our own good – even if we didn't always see her vision. Once we went to the Rand Easter Show, and Bokang took control of the money we had. She pooled it for transport then split the rest equally. I see the logic now but I also have to say that that was one of those shady older-sister moves ... Nonetheless, we had a good, safe, fun time!

That's who Bokang was then and who she is now: a protector and a leader who always has our best interests at heart. Bokang will fight for anyone she loves – literally. Bullies didn't stand a chance when it came to her siblings. She would fight on my behalf, but also with me! At home if I ever got on her nerves and she started to chase me around the house, I knew I would be in big trouble if she caught me.

She's an equal opportunity kind of person: anyone can be put in line, no matter what. She had this power because she was the one most closely tied to our centre of authority, our mother. If Bokang said, "Stop that or I'll tell Mama", she meant it. Mama would hear Bokang's opinion and act on it, too. My brother and I never wanted to hear that Bokang was going to tell on us. But, of course, among siblings everyone likes to see how or when they can get the other one in trouble.

We had our sibling ecosystem and we regulated it well.

When I was 16 years old, Bokang started university at VUT (Vaal University of Technology). With this new distance between us, our relationship changed from the strict boundaries of older and baby sister to more of a friendship between young women. We were each growing up and learning about ourselves, and that changed how we related to each other. Now, I feel like Bokang is my greatest supporter. She will drop anything for me and her guidance, especially recently with *Jesus This, Jesus That*, has been invaluable. Our relationship with Ntlafatso is amazing, especially now that he's in his early twenties. He's a well-spoken, intelligent young man.

We're a family who loves information; we'll watch the news or read the paper and then spend hours discussing what we've learned. The debates often get quite fiery – and it keeps us all sharp.

We all had good academics in common even as we each cultivated our own personalities and interests.

Where Bokang and my brother are more serious and they approach people and the world with logic and boundaries, I am the sister who crashes past rules and asks all the awkward questions. I'm the odd one out, the maverick, and I keep them on their toes.

Besides all the good-natured teasing and chaos, one thing is always true: we are a strong unit and we've been raised to have each other's best interests at heart. We look out for each other and love each other fiercely.

We are each other's number-one priority. A clear example of this was when, a few years ago after I had knee surgery, my family took turns living with me while I recovered. My brother would take me to work at Lesedi FM during those late hours, wait for me at the studio (catching a little well-deserved nap) and then take me home, making sure I was comfortable and fed. I never would have thought that our relationship would bring us there, but it did – and it's a product of how we were raised.

My mother has always been intentional about raising us to be tight-knit. And in 2020, when the world was in lockdown and everyone was re-evaluating what was truly important, my mom took the time to talk to us all and make sure we never forgot the importance of family.

It was strange hearing her get so serious on Christmas Day, but she was right to remind us that we must always support and love and protect each other. She told my brother, "Do you see how your sisters have each other's back? You have access to them – draw from that." To really drive her point home, she said, "I'm not going to be here forever; the three of you are what life has offered you. Nothing will replace this unit." And that's really the essence of it.

Now that we're older and I've interacted with different people through school and work, I've realised that the closeness I have with my siblings is not common. Sometimes I watch other siblings and it seems like they have their own separate lives. My brother and sister and I are very much in each other's lives. We are genuine friends. We go to concerts together, we spend holidays together. Spending time together doesn't feel uncomfortable, or like an obligation.

Bokang is the glue that holds us together in the sense that she's always reminding us to check up on each other. She guards and looks over the relationships, keeps us accountable to each other. And I follow that example by always forcing us to be in the same place: visits, outings, family gatherings, holidays. My responsibility is to make sure we spend time together, getting to know each other and our extended family.

All three of us grew up in the same world: moving between the Vaal and Qwa Qwa and Lesotho, interacting with different family members in their parts of the world. We each learned how to adapt to different environments, whether rural or urban, and we took the realities of life in our stride. We were never above using long-drop toilets or spending holidays in a place with little to no electricity or TV signal.

Thanks to our respect for time, connection and family, we knew how to stay humble and present – and our perspective of life and the world was deeper and better for it.

We have this beautiful relationship, the three of us, but we each relate to the other separately, differently. There is this world we inhabit together, and then this world that we experience with each other. We have a sibling code that allows us to keep each other on our toes while also helping us stay on our mother's good side; if she's got a bone to pick with one of us, we'll raise the alarm on the call and text chain so that whichever child's she's got in her sights is prepared. Like I said: we've always got each other's backs. I don't know what I would do without them!

I love being my mother's daughter, but I also love watching her be a daughter to her own mother. It is so satisfying, because I think, "Everything that irritates you about me, you are now experiencing with your own mom!" The dynamics between mother and daughter are the same across generations. Mothers want to know what you're doing, where you're going, when you're coming home for Christmas ... they are all the same. It's fascinating to watch how my mom is treated like the child of the house when we go and visit my grandmother in Lesotho. Her mother sends her on errands and scolds her over little things, making it clear that she – my grandmother – is in charge in her home. And that's family: we all know our place and how to make our world work.

The value of a friend

While family may be the first example of community with which we grow up, I also believe strongly that friends, chosen family if you will, are also brought into our lives to show us community and how they can enrich our lives.

I have had three friends walk very closely with me in this life and they've shown me what I believe are the three most important principles of enriching friendship: honesty, accountability and investment.

A value that I believe pushes through all areas of friendship is honesty. For a friendship to be strong, the people in it must be invested in telling the truth to each other, about each other's choices, feelings and plans. They must be ready to be radically honest, willing to confront uncomfortable topics, and be completely vulnerable with one another.

As people, we are quick to shy away from speaking about our weaknesses and limitations or those of others. But I believe the depth of friendship is best experienced if we really *go there* with each other. You must have people around you who will tell it like it is, even when you don't want to hear it. Good friends will celebrate you in a heartbeat, but will be just as quick to point out the excuses you're leaning on or warn you against making mistakes.

Eva and I had this kind of honesty in our friendship. Once we had left home, graduated university and started our "grown-up" lives, our schedules became fuller and it was more difficult to spend time together. We still had a very strong bond, but it was not the same and Eva was not comfortable with that, especially once she had identified me as the biggest culprit.

I was starting out in the entertainment industry, going wherever the gigs were and working incredibly long hours. This started to take a toll, and one day Eva confronted me about how unavailable I was. We had a huge fight and Eva landed her point with one question: "How do you expect me to know this new you that is evolving if you don't have time to see me?"

I was not present. I was calling less and, in that year, I had even neglected to celebrate Eva's birthday properly. The cracks were really showing, and I needed someone to point out what was really going on, before it was too late.

Naturally, no one wants to hear that they have failed their friend. We don't want to hear that we have disappointed the people we love. So, it was a difficult conversation for me, but I needed to hear the truth.

The truth was I had not learned how to balance my work life and my personal life. I had not found my feet in the fast-paced industry I had been thrown into. I was taking on more work and pushing my priorities – family and friends – further and further down the list. I was holding onto this new job and new world but letting other things slip. And it had serious consequences. I was starting to lose touch with my family, no longer giving them as much of me as I could or should have.

What Eva was showing me was that, yes, it was good that I was working hard, providing for my family and building a positive reputation in the industry – but I could not use all that as an excuse to not be present. I had stopped being a good witness in my people's lives, and that had to stop.

I tried to debate my way out of it, because of course no conversation between Eva and I could pass without some sparring. But in the end, there was nothing for it: Eva was right. When I thought about our confrontation later on, when I was alone, I knew that Eva was telling the truth.

Now more than ever, now that Eva is gone, I recognise that balance is key. With my family and even with myself, time is the most valuable gift I can give. Hearing that I was falling short was hurtful, especially coming from my best friend, who I would always give my all to.

What Eva said was not new to me, either: my mother had started the same conversation with me, too. When my mother said the same thing, I brushed it off, but when Eva said it, I really *heard* it. She was the closest person to me, someone who I had chosen to do life with, and so her message had impact.

That time in our lives was a test for Eva and me. Could we be fully honest and still not imagine our lives without each other? We landed at yes, and for that I am eternally grateful. It was that radical, loving honesty that deepened our relationship.

Friendships also thrive on accountability. We can look to 1 Timothy 4 again, where we find that Paul was laying out all Timothy's responsibilities as a believer and encouraging him to step up. In that example, accountability looked like re-examining the priorities of Christian life and committing to excelling – to being an example – in all areas.

Accountability is where the idea of "doing life together" comes alive. Stepping out in community to work towards your life's goals requires strong accountability partners; these are friends, mentors and like-minded people who we meet along the way.

Many of us run away from taking accountability because we are afraid of what we will see in the mirror that our friends hold up to our lives. In truth, if I hadn't had someone to support me and hold me to the promises I made to myself during that difficult period after my knee surgery, I would have not learned the lessons that that experience had for me.

In 2021, when I started filming a travel show with Absa, my friend Lesego was on the road with me as my make-up artist. This was when I had started physiotherapy to aid my recovery. I was working long hours, hobbling around on crutches and using all my energy to keep a positive attitude. By the time the day ended and we went home, all I wanted to do was sleep.

But not on Lesego's watch. We had spoken about my exercise schedule and, because she cared about my well-being, she took on the responsibility of getting me to do my stretches. She would not stand by and watch me ignore the biokineticist's instructions.

I was tired and in pain, with nothing to give. But Lesego would come into my room, pull out the exercise equipment and watch me do the stretches until I finished the day's required set. My mood was low, and after a day of struggling to not let the condition of my body get in the way of my work, I didn't want yet another reminder that I was in a wheelchair. But Lesego did not give up on me and she did not let me give up on myself. She forced me to stay accountable. She stood by me and did not allow me to wallow in self-pity. She enforced discipline and made me do what was best for my future. That's a true friend.

You need a friend who will be there to make sure you're doing well, or to even ask what's standing in the way of you doing it. And it's all done out of love.

Friends come in so beautifully to encourage us: start the exercise programme, read the chapter in your textbook, practise your craft. We want good friends but we also want friends who will offer us what we *need*. And that's what Lesego did for me.

Friends walk alongside you in all that you do, helping to clear the path for your success in all areas of life. In our current time of quick fixes and commitment phobia, I find that people are less and less willing to invest in one another. Friendships are built with effort and over time. Being a good friend means making a decision to give your time, energy and, ultimately, your love.

Investing in relationships means sticking around: staying by your friend's side after the first big fight, through career changes, through rough patches with family. Investing means committing to staying friends through all of life's seasons; being *consistent* and growing with your people. Investment in a friend means giving them a wider perspective on their life, examining their goals and looking at how you can help them be the best version of themselves. And it is done out of love and a genuine desire to see them succeed in life.

My manager, Sthe, and I have been friends since I was 18 years old. He was there to see me discover my place in the entertainment industry and, because he was able to see the vision, he decided to invest in my growth. He recognised my talent and skill and went about creating space for it to expand and develop.

When I was starting out, people working on television did not have managers, per se. We worked with agents, and that's how we would get our contracts. This is okay until you're getting more work and dealing with more serious clients. Then you need a real representative.

That's when my friend stepped up for me, and started managing the business side of my career.

While I was focused on building my portfolio and getting my name out there, he was focused on building a strong business foundation for me. Things like making me a rate card, writing me an official biography, getting me to invest in an official domain so that my emails to clients could be more professional, and changing my bank accounts to business accounts where necessary, all helped me to legitimise my work.

At every given chance, he would plug in to my work, thinking several steps ahead and making sure that I was on track to get to where he knew I belonged. He was investing in my future.

It's incredible to experience it from your chosen family, because it's the kind of love and care and encouragement that one might typically only expect from your biological family who are somewhat obliged to be there.

Community is a concept I grew up with; I was surrounded by strong friendships, family ties and mentorships while I was growing up, and I strive to maintain similar connections now. The key ingredient of community – and in this sense I am speaking specifically about friendship as community – is alignment.

In 1 Timothy 4, we find an example of friendship and mentorship, where Paul reminds Timothy of their shared values, of their common goals to work for the Kingdom of God. In my own life, I have found myself most aligned with people who share my common values of faith, love, kindness, family and discipline, among other things.

When we stand for the same things, it's easier for us to walk the path of life together.

Loving people as Jesus loves me

My first and most enduring example of love in action, when we are not talking about Jesus Himself, was my mother. Several times in my childhood, I saw her extending her time and resources to people in need and never once hesitating to improve someone's circumstances if she could.

I remember one particular incident on a day when my mom and I were travelling together on public transport, and she spotted a woman and her child looking a little lost. My mother engaged with her, asking where she was going and who was waiting for them on the other side. When it became clear that the young woman was going to be alone in an unfamiliar place, my mother decided to help her along and give her a safe place to land: our own home.

This was someone who we did not know at all, but my mother did not let that stop her from loving a stranger and opening her home to her. That night, the young woman and her child stayed in one of our bedrooms and some of us slept on the floor. The entire experience was a lesson in compassion and selflessness. It was how my mother lived out her faith and showed Christ-like love for her fellow man.

The story of Jesus with the Samaritan woman at the well in John 4 is one I turn to when I am looking for examples of how to love like Christ.

John 4:7-10 says: "When a Samaritan woman came to draw water, Jesus said to her, 'Will you give me a drink?' (His disciples had gone into the town to buy food.) The Samaritan woman said to him, 'You are a Jew and I am a Samaritan woman. How can you ask me for a drink?' (For Jews do not associate with Samaritans.) Jesus answered her, 'If you knew the gift of God and who it is that asks you for a drink, you would have asked him and he would have given you living water.'" (Amplified Bible)

This passage stands out boldly to me: the two of them, by the laws of the time, were expressly forbidden from interacting, let alone in public and at that specific time of day. The Samaritan woman was at the well during the time that "sinners" were given for drawing water; the Jewish people, who had been set aside as "righteous", would go when it was cooler outside. Jesus sees the woman and asks for a drink of water. She is shocked and reminds Him that they are from two groups who are not allowed to speak or share anything. Jesus crosses that boundary imposed by others and offers the woman Himself: He offers her living water. He speaks to her and advises her on how she can live a better life. The Samaritan woman is resistant and doesn't immediately believe that Jesus has anything for her, but He persists. He continues to love her.

He had put himself in danger, because the men in the area would not hesitate to harm anyone they perceived as an enemy. And today, that is what we think of first: our individual safety or convenience. We use that, and any real or perceived difference between ourselves and the person in need to judge them and to justify not reaching out.

When I study the story in John 4, I see that there can be no excuse for me, as a follower of Jesus, to not do as He has done, and love people, and give them whatever I can.

I have learned that I cannot withhold my love like that, especially when I am so clearly a product of people seeing me, reaching out to me, helping me. The English teachers, the staff at the restaurants where I worked, the debating coaches who spotted a talent in me and chose to nurture it, everyone who decided to open doors for me – these people did not look at my background or my age and use that to determine whether I deserved help or not. So, who am I to shy away from my responsibility to help? What's my excuse?

I believe it is the Holy Spirit who convicts me to step out of my comfort zone and help people who need it. How can I not assist someone when I myself have been so heavily assisted? I am here, where I am in my life, because I am a product of all the help and love and pushes of encouragement that I have received along the way.

I cannot shy away from my responsibility to help, and that is why I don't consider my own comfort over the needs of others in my daily walk through life.

One night, after hosting an Africa Day event at Constitution Hill, I was driving through Parktown on my way home and I saw a couple on the side of the road. As my headlights hit them, I realised it was a full family: two parents and about seven children. The eldest looked about 11 years old and the youngest couldn't have been much older than one.

I was immediately on high alert and I stopped, rolled down my window and asked them if they were okay.

One of the parents spoke up and asked if I could give them food. Seeing a family looking so destitute broke my heart and I knew I had to help. I drove to the nearest garage to buy them something to eat. While I was there, I realised that I should get help from someone. I decided to ask one of the neighbourhood patrol drivers for assistance, but they said they couldn't intervene because the family was out of their company's jurisdiction. I was told that the best they could do was drive behind my car and watch what happened from a distance.

So, I bought food and got back into my car. When I found the family again, they eagerly accepted the food and the children became a little more talkative, even speaking up to say, "Thank you, Aunty". At this point, I was fully invested in this family's wellbeing.

I told them that I'd like to check up on them and they said that they could meet me at a nearby mall. They said that they had a cell phone that they kept at someone's house, so I took their number and went home. The next day, I went to see them and we talked some more about how I could possibly help them. The next time I saw them, I was with my then-boyfriend, who was already sceptical of the situation because he knew my heart and how quick I was to get deeply involved with people.

We took the family to a Spur restaurant. Some of the patrons stared, of course, because here I had this dishevelled family in tow. I was trying to get to know them, and when they asked for more food to take away, I paid for it.

After that meeting I decided to rent a place for them. I paid three months' rent upfront and left them with a bit of money, saying I'd be back to check on them during the month. A short while later, they left the place without telling me why. Having them back on the outside didn't sound like a good idea to me because I could see that the children had rashes on their bodies. When I brought it up, the mother dismissed it, saying, "Oh, we sleep outside, you know how it is …"

The parents were adamant that I should not call social workers. "We don't want trouble, and you know the social workers would take the children away. We just want to find work." I didn't question them, but I became more aware that I needed help with the situation. That's why, when a woman from a local crèche, who knew a little bit about the family's situation because she worked in the area where they'd often spend the night, called to step in and say she had a room for them to stay in, I took her up on the offer. I had no choice at that moment: the woman from the crèche was reaching out because Veronica, the children's mother, had just given birth to a premature baby. I wasn't even aware that she was pregnant.

I'd already attempted to assist them with accommodation, and it was now a crisis. But in the end, they were committed to chaos: when I asked them why they had left the place I rented, they said it was difficult for them to "hustle" while they were there. That was the choice they were making: between having a roof over their heads and hustling for small amounts of money to stitch together their days.

Two weeks or so into the saga, the woman from the crèche called me and said she had officially got social workers involved. The woman said that she could see my efforts and knew that my heart was in it, but encouraged me to distance myself from the situation; it had turned into something much more than either of us could handle.

A grandmother, the man's mother, I believe, was called and she made a firm decision: she would take all the children – and she didn't want either of the parents near them again. After this, Veronica called me, angry and shouting, asking how I could approach the social workers. She also had her children send me messages saying, "Please don't let anyone take us away from our mother!"

At this point I was being seriously manipulated. My own mother advised me to step back and let social services take over. It was best for me to let the children go. I prayed about it – trying to understand all my conflicting feelings – and the answer was: "Let it go". And that was that.

I have learned that whenever you reach out to help someone, you've got to love people that much, but you've got to love God that much more, to believe in that moment that He's the one telling you to go somewhere and do something. It is, among other things, the practice of "love your neighbour as you love yourself". There's no time to ask should I, is it safe, can't someone else step in, what if something goes wrong. I can't answer those questions. But that can't be the reason I don't do what God tells me to do. Being in tune with that command from the Holy Spirit, that's the hardest part. And it can only come from relationship – real relationship – with God.

People can look at this situation and others in my life and say, "You've got such a good heart" – but it's all the will of God. It is all pure obedience. A so-called good heart can only go so far – after that, it's all God.

One day in winter 2022, when I was driving into Soweto for one of my regular meetings, I saw a group of grannies running on the side of the road. Naturally, I drove after them and I asked them what was going on. Why were these elderly women running? They told me they were in a running group; I was intrigued, and told them I'd be back to talk some more after my meeting.

I learned that they regularly ran together and then met up for a meal with Stella, a young woman from the area who made food for the women and helped them take their medicine. That was it for me: Stella was a girl after my own heart, and I wanted to help her!

I decided to go onto Instagram and reach out to Adidas, who I had a working relationship with at the time, and asked them to provide proper running shoes and clothes for the group. We ended up organising a clinic, where people from Adidas came and evaluated the women's needs so that they could provide the correct shoes. While I was waiting for a cheque to afford these shoes, I went back to Soweto every Monday, Wednesday and Friday to run with the gogos, getting to know them. This was never going to be a "drop off the gifts and leave" situation – I mean, have you met me?

I was seeing my running gogos regularly that winter, and I was doing my usual drive into Soweto on a misty morning when I noticed a girl and an older woman, who I assumed was her mother, on the side of the road. The older woman was lying down with a blanket over her body. I stopped to find out what was happening and that's when the girl, Mbali, told me she and her mother, who was incredibly ill, were waiting for an ambulance. They stayed in a nearby informal settlement called Tjovitjo, outside Freedom Park. They couldn't wait for an ambulance at home because emergency services didn't go into "unofficial" areas.

I helped the mother, Mam' Sithole, into my car, where I turned up the heater while I chatted to Mbali to find out more about the situation. All the while, I was praying. Seeing Mam' Sithole going in and out of consciousness raised alarm bells in my head and in my heart. The meeting I was supposed to have with the gogos was pushed aside in the midst of this emergency, but when the ambulance finally arrived, I let Mbali and Mam' Sithole go ahead, planning to check in on them later.

The running gogos and I had brunch and a catch-up and we were all in high spirits. This group of women and I were really becoming close friends. But elsewhere in the city, Mbali and Mam' Sithole were still in need of a helping hand.

I headed to Chris Hani Baragwanath Hospital in the early afternoon and found that, despite her serious condition and the hours that had passed, Mam' Sithole had still not been attended to. My diary was full that day, so I left to do a voice-over job. When I got back at around three in the afternoon, Mam' Sithole was still waiting. This is a woman who, due to her work as an informal recycler, frequenting dumping sites and regularly inhaling all sorts of toxic fumes, was now so sick that she was struggling to breathe. But she was still waiting at the hospital.

At around nine that night, after Mbali and I had waited so long that we had actually seen doctors changing shifts, Mam' Sithole was admitted and her daughter and I left the hospital. Now it was just me and Mbali in Tjovitjo at around 10 at night.

A few days later, Mbali, who has now become my responsibility, called me to say that she was worried: her mother was not looking well. When I got to the hospital,

I saw that Mam' Sithole's condition had worsened to a point where she was losing vision and couldn't recognise her daughter. I started to panic.

Knowing that Mbali was going to need all the help she could get, I asked if there was anyone she could reach out to. She said that she had an older sister in KwaZulu-Natal (KZN). I called the sister on Mbali's behalf and explained what was happening. The young woman was dismissive: she'd obviously cut ties with her family and didn't feel the need to immediately jump into action. Soon after this call, Mam' Sithole passed away. That was it for Mbali.

I learned that day that at Bara, if someone dies while they're admitted, the hospital gives their people a R700 stipend. So, it was me, Mbali and a dead body – and R700. I sat on those chairs and thought, "Lord, I have never seen anything like this before."

Mbali told me that she had some family, uncles, in Eswatini (Swaziland). We called them to tell them what had happened, and they said they would send money as soon as we told them what the plan was. They left the responsibility of burying the mother in the child's hands. Hearing that left me defeated.

But we had to keep on moving. We spoke to the staff at Bara and I explained that Mbali was now on her own, so they agreed to keep Mma' Sithole's body there for a few more days – an arrangement that could be nothing but temporary, because Bara's morgue also had its own space issues.

A day or two after Mam' Sithole's passing, my own mother came into town and I was so grateful to have her support while I was helping Mbali. She and Mbali were together for a while on a day when I had to leave Soweto for a work commitment. When I got back from work, I found that my mother had made a plan to move Mam' Sithole from Bara to a local Soweto mortuary, so we went to move the body.

At the Bara morgue, there's a big window that people can look through when they come to collect their loved ones. Standing there and looking in was just another one of the surreal moments of this ordeal. Three days in and Mbali, who was becoming more and more attached to me, was still a child with no family support in the middle of what was probably the most painful moment of her life.

The next thing we knew, the uncles in Eswatini were insisting that Mam' Sithole should be buried in that country. The logistics were a nightmare; neither Mbali nor Mam' Sithole were correctly documented, and there was no proper transport to take everyone over the border. But Mbali's uncles were nothing if not audacious: they arrived in Soweto at seven at night in an 11-seater van.

They informed us that they would be folding the seats down to fit in the coffin.

I was devastated. With the way I was crying, people would have believed that *I* was Mam' Sithole's daughter. Later Mbali told me how she and her sister, Sibongile, who only arrived on the day Mam' Sithole was being taken over the border, sat in the back, next to the coffin, all the way to Eswatini – when they arrived at the family home, they had to bury their mother immediately; they couldn't even take a bath first.

When I fetched Mbali at Park Station, she broke down and ran into my arms. If she hadn't been my child before that, at that moment I knew I couldn't let Mbali go. She was my responsibility, and still is even today.

Continuing my year of taking responsibility was Zanele. I met her around the time I met Mbali and in the same way that I'd met the family in Parktown: on a late-night drive back from work.

On Monday, Tuesday and Wednesday from midnight until two in the morning I was on-air at Lesedi FM, and again on Thursday and Friday mornings for the breakfast show. I used the graveyard shifts to practise my Sesotho and get used to presenting in the language, so that by the time I got to the desk on Thursday and Friday morning, I was comfortable.

I was on the way home from Auckland Park in the small hours of the morning when I saw a woman walking on the side of the road. It was dark and quiet, so I was bound to notice any small movements. I was now alert, and as I drove closer to the woman, who was walking in the opposite direction, I saw that there was a child on her shoulders. About 500 metres away I could see a man, and this woman seemed to be following him. I now knew that they were together, and I sensed that I must intervene.

It turned out they were walking towards Sontonga Road, an area I'm familiar with. I got to the gate of my complex on that road, asked the security guard to watch me and the car, and drove back out into the street to approach the woman. I got close to her, rolled my passenger-side window down and asked her what was happening. She was crying and barefoot; it was the middle of June.

She said, "I just had a fight with my boyfriend, bra". I was surprised to hear her speaking with a Joburg twang. I asked her where she was going and she said she was following him. I was now close enough to notice that her face was bruised.

I took out my phone and went live on Instagram, a safety measure I had recently adopted. I asked her name and she told me that it was Zanele. I said, "Zanele, I'm going to put you in my car". It wasn't because I had a plan, but I thought I could at least speak to her boyfriend.

Zanele and her child got into the car and I noticed that they were both not dressed for the cold. I started praying, "Father, please give us grace. I don't know what the situation is but I know that You are in control."

I parked just inside my complex gate, left Zanele and her child in the car, and went after the boyfriend. He was walking towards Fietas, one of Johannesburg's poorest suburbs, and I stopped him, saying, "Hi, I'm sorry but can I just talk to you? What's going on?"

He didn't answer and chose to swear at me instead. I continued walking behind him, trying to engage with him, but the security guard from my complex intervened and told me to leave the man alone.

I went back to the car and focused on what I could do for Zanele. First, I needed to get her and her son properly dressed. All the while, I was on Instagram Live. The three of us entered my house and I was speaking out loud, praying, trying to figure out what to do. I grabbed basic winter things I found around the house – jackets, blankets, whatever I could get my hands on that would keep them warm. For shoes, I gave Zanele a pair of Adidas sneakers that the company had given me when I worked on an activation programme; they happened to be in her size. While she was getting dressed, I noticed her movements were stilted, and not just from the cold. She was having difficulty bending to pull things on.

When I asked her, "Zanele, are you pregnant?", she said yes and started crying. I started crying too, right on Instagram Live. At this point, I had a woman who appears to have been beaten up by her boyfriend, a two-year-old child and a "surprise" pregnancy.

Zanele told me that she'd been on the streets for three weeks. Now, I know from picking up homeless people in the past that a person who has been on the streets has a certain smell about them; you can tell by looking at them how long they've been outside. I knew that Zanele was not telling me everything: to me, she looked like she'd been outside for months at least.

I was now on high alert, but I still had a situation to deal with.

The next step I took was to take Zanele and her son, Joey, to the police station, so they could be booked into a shelter for the night. I filled in the forms and the police told me to leave Zanele and Joey there; they'd have to wait until eight in the morning when the unit dealing with mothers and children on the street would open.

Because I was still worried about the pregnancy, I tried to get information from Zanele about when last she saw a nurse. She told me that it had been a few weeks since she'd had money to go to a clinic – but antenatal care is free to those who need it, so that was another false statement from her. I decided to level with her, saying that

I could only assist her up to a point if she didn't tell me everything. That's when Zanele finally opened up.

She told me that her boyfriend was on drugs and that he was abusive. She said that she was not on drugs, that she'd come to Johannesburg from Durban. The problems were clearly much deeper than I could have anticipated, but I was still intent on helping her. I left the two of them at the police station in search of food.

Leaving them at the police station overnight didn't feel right. I was still on Instagram Live and talking out loud, saying, "Holy Spirit, I can't take them home …" The people watching were stressed, commenting, "Don't take them home!"

Realising that I was close to Milpark Garden Court, I decided that it was my next best bet. I went over to the hotel and pleaded my case: "I don't know what your policies are, but I want to bring a homeless person and her child here to stay the night. I have booked them in at the police station but the office doesn't open until 08:00. If you let them stay, I promise I'll be back in the morning to fetch them."

Fortunately, the manager was willing to help. I paid for the night to show them that I was committed. I took the invoice with me to the police station. The people there were sceptical – they see these things go wrong all the time – but they let me leave with Zanele and Joey.

At the hotel, I told Zanele to get herself and Joey clean. They were both bruised, with blisters all over their bodies, and their hair was in a state. I knew that if I walked into the social services office in the morning with them looking that way, they would immediately take Joey away.

Before I left, Zanele said she was going to need nappies. I was surprised: was Joey not past that stage? But he was not, as Zanele had led me to believe, two years old and somewhat independent. Zanele was on the streets with a baby who had not been potty trained. Her situation was complicated by her half-truths and omissions. But my mission was not to judge her.

In the morning, after we signed back in at the police station, we were directed to a unit at Rahima Moosa Mother and Child Hospital. Myself, Zanele, Joey and an officer were going there in my car, because there were no vans available at the police station. This was truly the most adventurous 24 hours!

The revelations kept on coming: before the hospital could take people in at the boarding unit, they needed to check everyone's health status. During this test, I learned that Zanele had not been truthful about her pregnancy: she was in fact weeks away from giving birth. At this point, I believed Joey was born on the street, too, which confirmed my earlier suspicion that Zanele had been living on the streets for far longer than she'd said.

Over the next week, I was at the hospital during every free moment, checking on Joey and Zanele. The toddler, who had been hysterical upon being separated from his mother, had become calmer, and even recognised me when I visited.

The hospital's priority was getting Zanele strong enough to give birth. And she had to do that without Joey (because he was in the children's ward), so her anxiety was high. Especially since Joey was now seen to be malnourished and lacking in social skills, which brought up issues of neglect. Zanele pleaded with me to look after Joey for her, and I did – even sitting in meetings with hospital staff about his health. I was standing in the gap so that the social services professionals didn't immediately take the child away.

After some time, Zanele, Joey and her new baby were discharged. At this point I was cut off from communicating directly with them: social services took over.

With this, more information about Zanele's life came to light. I found out that, instead of the one four-year-old daughter she told me was living with her mother in KwaZulu-Natal, Zanele has four other known children, and they had all been taken into the system.

This, along with Zanele's description of how her relationship with her mother was nonexistent because she didn't agree with Zanele's "lifestyle choices", the fight with her boyfriend, and her habit of lying all showed me that this was a classic case of drug addiction. That's what was preventing this well-spoken, apparently smart young woman who was in her early thirties from getting and keeping a regular job.

A few months after the baby was born I was still in contact with social services. When Zanele applied for jobs, they contacted me to give a reference. The distance between us after that intense initial period was loaded, but this was not my first time so I was better at backing off and letting the system take over.

In each of these instances, I put my own comfort aside and focused only on helping these people in their time of need. I put my faith and my love into action, choosing to do what I believe Jesus would do.

I recognised a need and I felt convicted to help. Where there were challenges, I let the Holy Spirit guide me to a solution. At every turn, I did my utmost to demonstrate Christ-like love, to not let any notion of a "comfort zone" stop me. Naturally, I was afraid and frustrated at many points. And I was aware of people close to me and those following the stories that I would share on social media advising me to be careful of getting too involved or, in some cases, to "leave things to the authorities". A person's first instinct is to protect themselves. What's more, there's the simple idea that no one wants to be taken advantage of. These are all the things that could have held me back.

Bu there's one thing, one truth, that is stronger than these doubts: when I don't help wherever I feel compelled to do so, I am being disobedient to God. I am the one who is wrong for holding out on sharing my resources – time, shelter, clothing, money – with those who God brings along my path. When God has allowed me to steward something, when He has given me a gift, I am accountable to Him for how I use it. *I* am the one who has to answer for what I decided to do with my gifts.

The same is true for the people you or I choose to help: they will be accountable to God for how they receive and use the gifts – that is, the different kinds of help – that are given to them. So, while people may question why I would help people who are "beyond help" or who are "ungrateful", I know that I have protected my heart with the knowledge that I have done my best to obey God's commands and one day we will all have to answer for our choices and behaviours.

Another safeguard is to be honest in your approach and to really examine what's really going on in your heart when you give. Are you giving with a grateful heart? Are you helping the person because they need it, and without expecting to glorify yourself? Are you giving with the awareness that you yourself have been helped along the way, and you're grateful for it?

In Mark 11:25 the Lord says: "And when you stand praying, if you hold anything against anyone, forgive them, so that your Father in heaven may forgive you your sins."

It is an opportunity for us as Christians to check ourselves and evaluate where our actions and motivations are coming from, remembering always that we help because we have been helped, we show compassion and empathy because it was first shown to us.

Imagine what life would be like if Jesus held back from helping and saving us because we were ungrateful? We cannot claim to be more deserving or righteous than the next person.

This perspective, that offering assistance is done with a grateful, compassionate heart and not with the expectation of reward or glory, is what supports my decisions to give of myself to improve the circumstances of others.

At each of the moments in the stories you have read, I felt compelled to help and I am grateful that I could. By the grace of God, I was able to make a real difference to these people's lives.

* Please note that we changed people's names in this chapter to protect their identities.

Eye on the prize: dating, marriage and everything in between

If there's one statement that is totally nonsensical to me, it's that favourite line of society's Marriage Police: "If you don't find someone and settle down, *you're going to die alone.*"

It's supposed to scare people – women especially – into rushing into getting married. It approaches the topic of marriage from the wrong place, as if it is some sort of qualifier of a "good" life. In reality, getting married is not the end goal. For me, the end goal is to have served the Lord well and to receive the promised reward in heaven.

I cannot be bated into believing that, because I am over the age of 30 and unmarried, there's something "missing" in my life. What I believe is that my God is faithful: He has the ability to fill my life with all that I need for whatever season I'm in. I am not in a rush for a husband, especially if it isn't someone sent directly from God.

I'm a relationship girl in a world where "casual dating" is the order of the day. While other people choose to cycle through potential partners in search of The One,

I favour a slower, more considered (and perhaps less popular) approach.

I take my guidance from 1 Timothy 4: "Be pure in your heart". This means being honest and intentional in all my interactions.

In the past, I have been upfront about certain things: I am a Christian; I am staying a virgin until marriage; I take my relationships very seriously. I always say to someone who wants to date me that the first three to six months of us knowing each other is a probation period. During this time, the two of us can get to know each other: talk about our goals and values, see if we have the same ideas of fun, learn if we approach the world the same way. And it gives time for those three important declarations to shake out and settle: after three months, if either one is unsure of whether they can stay celibate, or whether he even likes me as a person, I can release him with love.

Looking at my work in the public eye and the types of spaces in which I move, people assume that I'm dating all the young up-and-comers. In reality, I prefer to be friends with people before I consider anything romantic. All the people I have dated are people who have been in my life in one way or another. Though these people know something about my life, they are not always perfect partners and they do test my boundaries.

There was a producer from Nigeria who I had a working relationship with for some time. At one point in 2018 he started turning up the charm, asking me out and trying to get me to let my guard down. During one of these conversations, he probed the virginity topic, asking me, "How far do you go?" and attempted to engage me in a discussion of foreplay. I knew that I had to be firm about my convictions and why I had chosen to follow God's teachings very closely on this. That Nigerian producer, fellow Christian as he was, stopped talking to me soon after I told him that I was remaining a virgin until marriage. When people fall away like that it can be disappointing, but I have learned to just let them go.

In all interactions since then, I have been upfront about being a born-again Christian, and how it changes what is permissible and not permissible in a relationship with me. I also learned that meeting someone in a church environment or knowing someone as a self-proclaimed Christian does not guarantee that we will be on the same page about dating.

My slow and quiet approach to dating has allowed me to observe some things about men. Notably, I have learned that they have volatile emotions: just as women are judged for being "moody", men go through times where their emotions are high and their behaviour is unreasonable. This is when they are difficult to be with, when they are likely to give up on our arrangement. It's a "breaking point" of sorts. For someone else, that kind of behaviour from a man they are dating, that intense energy with which that man will try for sex, might be where things go wrong. It's easy to be manipulated by someone you have strong feelings for. By God's grace, I have learned how to take those feelings out of the equation and focus only on my goal, which is to serve God fully with my mind, soul and body.

When I was younger, I had a boyfriend who would break up with me every December. Things would be going well between us, but in December he would suddenly need to be "alone". I eventually realised that he left me over December so that he could date other people, and then in January he would come back and plead with me for the relationship to start up again. This kind of behaviour proved that I needed to stand by my convictions; I'd seen what unstable perspectives of oneself and of the purpose of relationships could do.

Along my intentional dating path, I have met people with whom I have a lot in common: men who enjoy art and travel and music. Through work, I am approached by people who claim to be interested in being in a relationship with me.

Some years into my career, when I was producing

a segment related to *Idols* for *Good Morning Africa*, I met and interviewed Musa Sukwene, who had recently won the national singing competition. We had music in common (at the time, I was singing with Muzart and our band was gaining popularity, having recently caught the attention of the South African Music Awards), and I was open to being friends.

For a while after our first meeting, we were friends, just getting to know each other. Over about eight months I watched his life, becoming familiar with how he thought.

He would say early on that he wanted to pursue a romantic relationship with me. He stated that my boundaries were exactly what drew me to him; my requirements put him in a position where he had to learn new ways to love someone, and he welcomed the challenge. That was what convinced me to give it a chance.

Ultimately, we were not compatible and we parted amicably. It was one of my longest relationships, and I believe it taught me a lot about myself and about what I wanted from a future partner.

At this point I must pause to say that I've learned a lot about how the modern dating scene pushes men to behave. The emphasis is on men being relentless in the pursuit of women – first, many of them, and then the one they want to marry. Men are told, at every turn, that they must make money and secure power, because this is what makes them "real men". It's as crude as that. Knowing this and realising the strain that it puts on potential relationships, I can empathise with men's dating experiences. They have been told that money and sex are the only ways they can show love.

With all this in mind, I take the feelings of the men I get into relationships with into consideration. Between their feelings and my own likes, dislikes and boundaries, I have been able to keep relationships going over time, with the longest one being about three years. Christianity sets it up that way for me; there can be no "talking stage" or "we're just going with the flow": it is serious from the beginning.

Recently I've had the idea that people who are dating should also go through counselling, similar to couples who plan to get married. If you're in a relationship and you intend to take it seriously, you should be talking to an elder in your church or a counsellor about how to direct your path. Ask all the difficult questions, such as gender roles in the home, and culture and money habits.

We must discuss what it means to show respect for each other, what it means to be in partnership, what a wife is, what a husband is. Do we agree on what it means to provide? Every thorny issue should be laid out on the table and given due attention.

The best way to prevent crucial mistakes is to approach

the relationship with intention and discipline; this will also prevent you from making decisions out of excitement. In dating, people have so many expectations that are based on fantasies created through media. A relationship with God will make you quickly realise that what you dream of for your relationship is not always real or good for you.

Do I want kids and marriage? Absolutely! But more than that, I want God to use me for the glory of His Kingdom. I don't want anything that's not what He has in store for me.

People have conflated marriage with sex in a way that is causing many to stumble. If getting married is viewed as the last "obstacle" before sex, then the many layers of life and learning that are tied up with marriage are ignored. In the church, people are told to wait for marriage, wait for marriage – but not to truly value marriage for what God says it is. The teachings lean heavily on Paul's writings in 1 Corinthians 7:9 (NKJV) – "But if they cannot control themselves, they should marry, for it is better to marry than to burn with passion" – and this skews everyone's perspective on marriage and what its purpose is.

I believe that people who are unhappy in their marriages are people who went into the arrangement before truly knowing themselves. They've become husbands, wives, moms, dads – and they are now filled with deep regret.

Because here's the thing: after the moment of "I do", there is real life. The two of you have to live together, in each other's space, sharing time and feelings and a future. If you don't know yourself, how can you hold space for the other complete human being in the relationship? This is why God must be at the centre, so that you have guidance and you pursue marriage for reasons more than just "I love him/her". Is it a godly love? A sacrificial one? One based on service? These are the important questions.

To young people who feel worried about missing out or are being told that it's "too late" to still hope that someone will marry them, I say: Don't disqualify yourself. As a Christian, you know that it is God who qualifies you for all work and blessings and positions in your life. You must not doubt this.

The Bible says "consider it pure joy" (James 1:2): your challenges, your job, your history, your achievements, your ambitions. Consider the *quality* of your life right now: How are you measuring it? Not by whether you are married or have had a child, surely. Not when you have so much more than that to your name.

In my mind and in my heart, I do have a desire for marriage and motherhood. Me being a virgin doesn't mean I disregard those things altogether. I look forward to the day God says to me, "This guy that you've been dating? Guess what: this is the one for you. Take care of each other." I would be so excited to hear that! But until then, I will keep walking close to God; that is my priority in this life.

Because of my personality, my life experiences, my faith, I have become a person who values marriage but does not put it on a pedestal. I understand it as the gift and blessing it is, especially when I consider that the Bible describes it as the illustration of God's love for His people. We, the church, are the bride, and Jesus is the perfect bridegroom who is waiting on us.

In dating I don't prioritise marriage. In the past, when people I have parted ways with have come back, asking for another chance and claiming to want marriage, I have not been moved. To me, it seemed that the men were using marriage as a bargaining chip, believing that making a promise would get me to lower my guard. But a false promise does not impress me, because I know how serious marriage is and I don't believe it's something that can be entered into lightly.

I can confidently say that my life is full, even without marriage or children. There is nothing "missing" from me. I will not "die alone". I did have a moment when I was younger where I thought that perhaps I had "waited too long", but now I realise that I'm not ready to settle down.

I have realised that the value of my life is in connections and community. I cannot die alone when I've been living a big, busy, beautiful life serving God and bringing people along with me on that journey. These are the people I am doing life with, the people who will be there until the end.

Dying "alone" is, from my perspective, a testament to the life you have led: who you loved and how well, the legacy you built for your people. It's not a spouse who could be estranged from you, or the number of children you have. If you're "alone" at the end, you were likely alone all along, not a sharer, a giver, a community member. So, when people talk about ending up alone, I invite them to think about what they are truly saying about themselves and their own lives.

If we truly look at marriage the way God intended it, we see that it is one of the greatest sacrifices a human being can make. In Ephesians 5:25 God says, "Husbands, love your wives, just *as Christ loved the church* and gave himself up for her" (my own ephasis) – meaning, have the willingness to die for them; have *unconditional* love. And women are called to "submit", to yield themselves to this other person completely. This is a very, very difficult thing to do. Which is why when people say, "When will you settle down?" or "A nice girl like you should have been married a long time ago!", I always think, it's got nothing to do with being nice. Marriage is serious business.

And in this world, life, as we know, is brutal. It is not something that can be done without a plan; marrying someone is for life, raising children in a dangerous world is for life. So, while I would love to have my own family one day, I am not in any rush to do something I don't feel ready for. I'm not in a perpetual state of "When is it my turn?" – that kind of worrying is just not useful to me.

I am eternally grateful that if it should happen, marriage for me will be in my latter years, because I have had time to experience my life, learn about myself, and become confident in my relationship with God. I needed that.

How I hold myself accountable in my faith

In the book of 1 Timothy, what we find is Paul the apostle sharing the Gospel with Timothy from the position of a teacher and mentor, with what I see as the tone of a caring, more experienced older brother. Paul's voice is stern and firm as he writes to Timothy and the church, giving them guidance based on his own life's lessons:

> *Don't let anyone look down on you because you are young, but set an example for the believers in speech, in conduct, in love, in faith and in purity. Until I come, devote yourself to the public reading of Scripture, to preaching and to teaching. Do not neglect your gift, which was given you through prophecy when the body of elders laid their hands on you. Be diligent in these matters; give yourself wholly to them, so that everyone may see your progress. Watch your life and doctrine closely. Persevere in them, because if you do, you will save both yourself and your hearers.*
>
> 1 TIMOTHY 4:12-16

In 1 Timothy 4, Paul is addressing a young person like me, that is, a young person who loves God and wants to be used by Him, someone who wants to participate in Kingdom things. The passage speaks to all the things that people believe make them unworthy or unqualified. Where Paul says in verse 12, "Don't let anyone look down on you because you are young …", I believe "young" can be substituted for any limitation that you put on yourself, or that society imposes on you: too short … too young … too big, not smart enough, strong enough, loud enough. Whatever that block is, that's what Paul is addressing. He is bringing up the innermost fears and insecurities that have been imposed by others, and letting Timothy know that these are not a reason to hold back. Paul is saying that there is no reason under the stars why Timothy should feel discouraged and be limited from doing the work of the Lord. There is no excuse.

Paul does not say to Timothy, "Ignore the naysayers"; he says that Timothy should not *allow* what is being said to take root, and that he should call it out immediately. Paul says you should never be in agreement with the limitations that society tries to impose on you.

Many of us tap out of our God convictions, promises and mandate over our lives because of societal and self-imposed standards that convince us that we are disqualified from being used by God.

In reality, God *qualifies* us, and nothing can change that. We can look to Romans 5:1, which says: "Therefore, since we have been justified through faith, we have peace with God through our Lord Jesus Christ." In relation to what Paul is saying to Timothy, this is a further affirmation that the standards of the world are not yours to take on.

Live in the reality that God has justified you. God has called you and qualified you – accept that and order your steps accordingly.

I also relate it to Ephesians 2:10, which tells us: "For we are God's handiwork, created in Christ Jesus to do good works, which God prepared in advance for us to do." We hear that we are justified and that we are God's handiwork (or workmanship); it has all been declared in advance for us, and there is so much beauty in knowing that God has planned it like that.

The confidence in the pre-existing plan is why Paul, after telling Timothy what *not* to do, starts his advice in verse 12 with but: "… but set an example for the believers". Here he means: with the knowledge that you are qualified by God through Christ, this – what he says next – is how you should behave. Paul says "do not", then uses "but" to signal to the reader to pay attention. The second part of the verse says, "but set an example for the believers in speech, in conduct, in love, and in purity."

For me, this is also a demonstration of how God is faithful enough to tell us what we *should not* be doing and to let us know what we *should* rather do, what we must do, and this is clear in many passages of the Bible.

For example, Joshua 1:9 tells us: "Be strong and courageous. Do not be afraid," which relates to our conduct as believers. And in Ephesians 4:29 a command about speech is found: "Do not let any unwholesome talk come out of your mouths, but only what is helpful for building others up according to their needs, that it may benefit those who listen."

And Paul speaks in this same instructional, disciplinarian tone of do this, not that; watch out for this, be aware of that. He introduces those five important areas of Christian life – speech, conduct, love, faith and purity – that Timothy should be diligent about. Paul says what not to do but also gives clear instructions on what you should do. It's straightforward, encouraging and loving, and for me that's what makes it one of the most beautiful passages in the Bible.

At this point in 1 Timothy, we have heard what *not* to do and what *to* do, and now the question of "how to do it" comes into play.

I believe that, as Christians and God-loving people, we mean well; we want to do good, but we get stuck at *how* to do it. In this part of Scripture, Paul gives Timothy a breakdown of how to set an example. It's not open for interpretation, it's not vague. Paul is directly talking about how to live in the reality of being God's workmanship.

It stresses that we should be an example, in all areas. In faith, in leadership (that is, conduct), in speech. And this passage also encourages spending more time reading the Word because it prompts you to look in the Bible for examples of faith, love, purity, speech and conduct. In studying it, the question becomes, "Am I being a good example?"

Paul believes that you can be. He is speaking directly into that part of our hearts that yearns for guidance and encouragement, reminding us that God has confidence in us.

I think Paul answers "the how" so beautifully, giving pointers on where you can start to check yourself. It is, if you look at it closely, self-explanatory; but it is not so simple to truly live out the words that Paul gives us.

For me, the wonder of this passage is in the clarity of the instruction: after reading this, you can make no mistake about what God expects of Christians. And all this is given in love; Paul is saying that we must know who we are in Christ and *decide* to step up and live the right way.

It is one of the first verses I learned by heart and so it is also one of my earliest touchpoints. It grounded me in my faith and became my reference point. Specifically, because I learned it when I was young and I was starting to express my love for Jesus in public, I latched onto that first part: "Do not let anyone look down on you because you are young". The verse reassured me that I was in the right place, doing the right thing. It gave me confidence that what I was doing, from taking my mother's Bible with me to school in Grade 2, to promoting myself to "big church" and going on missions, was normal. In this passage I found the directives needed to keep my path straight.

As I got older, I leaned into the second part of the Scripture. Paul is speaking to Timothy as a mentor and the discussion is about steps to live out your faith: your speech matters, how you love matters, how you live out your faith matters, purity matters. Paul was making sure there was no room for confusion.

When I say the Scripture is my touchpoint, I mean that I use it to hold myself accountable and to check myself when I am receiving feedback from the world about my faith journey. In my decision to remain a virgin, for example, there's an opportunity for me to check myself: yes, I am abstaining from sex and that immediately gives people the idea that I am "pure"; I am congratulated for it at MC gigs and my decision is glorified whenever I speak at events. But is virginity the "purity" Paul is talking about? Is he placing it on a pedestal? No. Paul's instruction is for believers to have a pure *heart*. I cannot be content that I am a virgin, I have to do more.

Staying a virgin is what's *expected* of me as a follower of God. It's not the reason for me to see myself as "better" than others.

With that Scripture in mind, I started to understand that God requires purity in mind and in action. The Bible says in Psalm 24:3, 4 "Who may ascend the mountain of the Lord? Who may stand in his holy place? The one who has clean hands and a pure heart …" I can be a virgin but not have a pure heart, I can be a leader at church but not be pure in thought or have pure intentions. If you're not pure in heart, it means you have forgotten where you received your salvation.

And that is also what this passage should remind us of: our hearts and minds should always be oriented towards God, and we should not neglect our responsibilities. In our society when Christians do the "obvious" things – no drinking, no smoking, no partying, no sex – they fall into the trap of thinking they are right with God. They feel like they've done everything they "should", and this leads to a sense of the entitlement in their relationship with God.

I remember when I realised this about myself. I was in hospital, going through a difficult period with my health. Me: a person who had been walking so closely to God all her life. Surely I had done enough to avoid this kind of suffering? But that's when I had to remember grace; it was through grace that I had made it to that point, not through my own strength. I had to purify my perspective on the situation.

Furthermore, there is obedience, and understanding that its true benefit is strengthening my relationship with God, not in the "rewards" for following instructions. I was not walking with God so that He could give me things in return or so that He could make my life easier than anyone else's. Through this Scripture and with the backdrop of this major life event, I had to re-examine my understanding of obedience. It is for us. In the same way that a child is warned against putting their hands on a hot stove plate or putting their fingers into an electrical socket – it is for their own safety and it is said out of love, but if they disobey, it is not the parent or guardian who will bear the consequences.

In reading this passage there is the opportunity to re-evaluate your priorities: Is there an area in your life that you are focusing on the most, and can you see that it is to the detriment of other important things?

The aim is to keep all five areas – speech, conduct, love, faith and purity – in mind; to work at all of them, so that when the world looks at you, they see an example of a faithful servant of God.

It is an instruction to be an example to believers specifically, which tells me that these verses are a strong charge. Being an example to Christians within the church, where there are factions and where people judge each other and there's competition to be the "perfect" Christian, is very difficult. But this must not stop you, a Christian, from doing what is right: "Don't let anyone look down on you" – always strive to live out what God has put in your heart, and don't be discouraged.

If I doubt my abilities or pass on opportunities because I feel I'm not good enough, I am looking down on myself *and* the talents and gifts God has given me. According to the Scripture, I cannot dare do that. In those human moments when self-doubt kicks in, I remind myself of this passage and check my actions against it: reading Paul's words and reaffirming that I am exactly who God wants me to be.

I believe that the culture of perfection stands in the way of hearing what God is truly asking us to do. As Christians, we choose one thing on which to focus all our energy – serving in the church, working for charities, keeping ourselves as virgins, excelling at work, etc. – and make that the area of "perfection". In reality, the only thing we should be focused on is God because He says

He will perfect all that concerns us (Psalm 138). He's not saying we should present ourselves as perfect; He's saying He will transform us.

The focus should be on the Word of God as a whole, because studying it will make it easier for you to live this life of faith because you will have a strong base. This passage from 1 Timothy tests your faith. It calls Christians to ask God, "How can I grow?" And it helps you to stay strong during the times when life is not going your way, when the temptation to crumble is nearly irresistible. In those moments, hold on to Paul's words instead of staying away from church and holding a grudge against God.

I am so grateful that in 2023, when my lifelong best friend Eva passed away, God put me in a position where I needed to speak about Him more and more. Through the Instagram Bible studies and *Jesus This, Jesus That*, God was speaking through me and healing me at the same time. His Word became my reality: I was reminded that God has promised me a future, that He gives me hope, that He is still my Father, that He still cares.

The events in my life at the time pushed me deeper into Bible study; they forced me to trust God and have faith in Him, even when I didn't want to.

It is deeply challenging to live your life according to 1 Timothy 4:12. It is really, really challenging, because you're not doing it for you. It is one of the biggest commands that make up the basis of Christian life: "die to self". Don't do it for you, do it as an example for other believers who are saved. Through salvation, show others what life is like with Jesus Christ.

The passage is a good place for anyone on their faith journey to begin because it sets the tone. It lays out your responsibilities and shows you your place in the culture of believers. You must be like Timothy. You must be like Paul. You must aspire to be like Christ. It's a great place to start.

The passage orients your heart to God and helps you, as a Christian, to avoid putting yourself over God and His Word. Often as Christians we think to ourselves: how do *I* look? Where do I fit in? How can I get a reward? What we should be focusing on is: Can people see God in me? Do my actions show it? Do my words show it? Does my mind show it? Are there things that I do that make my neighbours say, "Yes, that is a woman of God", before I ever tell them I am Christian?

We must aspire to be instantly recognisable Kingdom People: the Bible says, "you will know them by their fruit". Through studying Scripture and living it out, we should cultivate a spirit that is unmistakably good and faithful, and therefore inspiring.

A mistake we make is believing that we have to go through life in our own strength. The truth is that God is the One who gives us grace and empowers us to live the Christian life. This passage, along with others that give instructions for walking with God, is the reassurance that you do not have to do it alone.

You know what God has called you to do; now do it at a higher level, and hold yourself to a higher standard.

The passages say be pure in your speech. For me, that is about the declaration of faith. Getting comfortable speaking about God and settling into my faith – things that I was doing from a very young age. This Scripture is proof that I have been following in the footsteps of the believers who come before me. It's also about how you navigate the world as a Christian, how you answer the questions that are thrown at you. When people doubt that I am "really a virgin", when they question why I go out of my way to help people in need, when they say I can't be Christian *and* work in the entertainment industry – how do I answer them?

That's where guidance from this Scripture comes in.

Some Christians misuse the Word of God to a point where they don't sound relatable, or they lose the attention of the people they are speaking to. They pluck out certain Scriptures and force them into someone's space, not realising that people don't get saved because they've had Scripture thrown in their faces. People can tell if the preaching is not genuine.

When we go out as Christians aiming to be "fishers of men" (Matthew 4:19), we must be mindful of how our speech and actions align and what message they are sending.

If there's one thing 2023 taught me, it's that people are always watching you. Yes, I have been on television for many, many years, but I was introduced to a new level of scrutiny after I stepped out in faith, did this work that the Lord put on my heart, and watched the project grow and grow beyond what I could have imagined. I had to lean on the tenets in 1 Timothy 4:12 and stay pure in everything I did, so that *Jesus This, Jesus That* could do its intended work in the world.

In my time working in churches, and for the greater "church" as the community of believers in Christ, I have seen a tendency among us to be "checklist Christians". We go to church, we read the Bible, we participate in cell groups, and we tick all of these things off as "good" and "right". We reward ourselves for meeting these require-ments, forgetting that God is the rewarder. He is the One who can tell us whether we have done well or not. We put ourselves on pedestals and pat ourselves on the back, acting high and mighty and forgetting that it is by grace that we are saved. It is by grace that we are even given access to God – it's not due to any deserving of our own.

Many of us came into Christianity because we needed God to do something for us. We came to God as a performer, as a kind of Father Christmas who only exists to give us what we want. It's transactional, and that is the flaw in the approach. Instead of building a relationship and focusing on growing in obedience, we give God KPIs (key performance indicators). We list all the things we want, and say that we will pray and tithe until we get them.

We don't go to Him as a God, we don't go to Him as a Father. We don't go to Him as a saviour or a king. We go to Him as a connection who's going to help us get what we want.

This is not the way that we should be approaching our walk with God. We want to be seen and heard, we want our presence to be felt, which is why when God doesn't perform for us, we feel that He is jeopardising our reputation.

A relationship of trust and obedience allows us to understand the solemnity of the choice to follow God, and therefore the responsibility we have to walk the talk according to what's written in His Word.

"I put life and death before you" – God does not force us to do things His way. However, He does expect us to behave in a certain way once we have decided to align with His desires for our lives.

We must move away from the checklists and put God back in the centre. We can't create this perfect world where when people look at us, it feels like Christianity is unattainable. For one thing, self-edifying behaviour is not of God. It also keeps us in a disobedience loop, preventing us from truly progressing in our walk of faith. We as Christians need to take a step back and re-evaluate where our hearts truly are.

The performative nature of church culture is something that does not sit right with me. While faith without works is dead, these "works" must be based in biblical teaching and not in popularity contests. With God at the centre and with genuine intentions to live according to Scriptures such as 1 Timothy 4:12, the urge to perform extravagant "goodness" decreases. The drive to be a true example and to remove yourself from the centre of the church and Christianity conversations should be the most important thing.

Faith is strengthened through trial

For much of my life I have been a public figure, that special kind of character that people don't regard with the same rules of privacy. When you are in front of the mic or the camera every day, connecting with audiences, people think that they know you. I have learned to create boundaries between myself and the audience, and I do prefer to keep some of the more personal details of my life private. When questions are asked about my family, my relationships or my health, I give a high-level summary. I don't want to invite scrutiny and its close friend, unsolicited advice. I have found that, however "well-meaning" people may be, they are not entitled to some parts of my life. With respect, the only opinions and advice I take are from my family and my God.

With that said, I do also believe in honesty and integrity, and in the power of personal testimony. That is why I want to share the story of my journey with chronic illness.

From as far back as 2015, I have experienced phases of unexplained pain in my body. I presented myself to medical professionals who, as time wore on, prescribed more and more medication but could not reach a definitive diagnosis. By 2019, pain was a familiar part of my life, one I did not even discuss as an immediate problem any more. I am sure many people reading this will relate to the experience of suffering stoically to keep the show – work, family, life – on the road. I have contracts to honour, a household to maintain. If I need to take painkillers in order to do that, so be it.

At that point, I had not yet been given a clear prognosis, so I had no way of know what was in store.

I was on a job in 2019 when a colleague of mine complained of bad shoulder pain. I accompanied him to the doctor and, while we were travelling there, I sympathised with him. I shared how, for quite some time, I had been experiencing pain similar to and sometimes worse than what he had described that afternoon.

He took this conversation into the consulting room with him, presumably because the relative seriousness of it made the topic stick in his mind. I don't know exactly how my issues came up when he was talking to his doctor, but the next thing I knew, she walked out into the reception area, called me into her office, and sat me down for a conversation that would turn out to be life-changing.

I explained to the doctor – a black, bald-headed woman with an attitude that was both friendly and no-nonsense – about the several doctors who had sent me from pillar to post, drawing blood and doing scans. She said, "And no one has sent you to a gynaecologist?"

She wrote me a referral to one of her colleagues, and I left that office a little confused but no less open to seeing yet another doctor than I had been before.

But this was not going to be yet another doctor; the day Dr Sindi van Zyl (may she rest in peace) referred me to Dr Pule changed the trajectory of my healthcare journey.

After years of trying to make sense of what was going on in my body, I met with a doctor who was determined to take the time to find a solution that would not leave me at the mercy of nurses and pharmacists. Beween Dr van Zyl and Dr Pule, I also learned a lot about how differently black women experience the healthcare system, at all its levels, especially if they don't know how to advocate for themselves.

Through a combination of reassessing my medical history, talking to me about the details of my experience with pain, and a genuine interest in my wellbeing, Dr Pule reached the conclusion that I had chronic endometriosis and a case of polycystic ovarian syndrome (PCOS). Finally, the pain had a name. But that turned out to be just the beginning of this new chapter in my life. There was the adjustment to new cocktails of medication and the multiple surgeries between 2019 and 2021.

I was living in a very sick body and that knowledge deeply, deeply challenged my faith. I was walking close to God, trusting Him, praising Him, knowing that He was a God of healing. I was preaching to everyone about His goodness all the time, even during that initial period of illness and pain. But this advanced diagnosis put me in a new position regarding the Word and God. It was a time of deep uncertainty and even fear. I had to examine what my faith truly meant to me in a situation where I felt my body was betraying me; the evidence of my weakness was tangible. I was in unfamiliar territory. And still, that was not the deepest part of the valley.

Shortly after I started to properly process the prognosis from Dr Pule, I had another major health incident. During a charity netball match hosted by Joyous Celebration, I was tackled – because this was the kind of fun, loose game that didn't follow the conventional rules of the sport – by a male player from the other team. In the tussle, he fell on me, and I fell on my knee. I went off the court to put some ice on it and at the end of the match when my team was celebrating their win, I tried to get up to join them but the pain in my knee was very bad and I realised that something was wrong. A friend called a car to get me to a nearby casualty ward; at this point I still believed that all I needed was a strong painkiller.

A while later, after initial scans had been done on my incredibly swollen knee, a doctor who I would learn was an orthopaedic specialist, came in to explain that my knee was badly broken and I would need surgery to insert plates and bolts to rebuild it.

I was a person who lived with pain and had become accustomed to rating the severity of what was happening in my body on a sliding scale. I learned to ask myself questions like, is this an everyday pain? Is it a more intense pain? Is it an intense pain that I have felt before, or is it new?

If I find myself at a more severe level than usual, then I need to take myself to a hospital. And when I get there, because of my experience, I can tell the nurses what to give me, calling the medicine by name.

Now, after what was supposed to be a fun game between friends, I was told that another part of my body had essentially given up. Hearing about the surgery and going in for that procedure must look, to people who have not experienced it, like the most overwhelming part of the ordeal. But what I would learn is that it's the waking up after the surgery and having to leave the hospital and live with this new reality – that's the really difficult part.

At a time when I already felt my body was betraying me, this had me frustrated, asking what else could possibly go wrong. I was on the cusp of a new independence, having just moved into my new home, planning to decorate and renovate. Now I was thrown into a deep vulnerability, a kind of helplessness that was foreign to a hyper-independent person like me. I had to fight my way out of that. The security I had created for myself was under threat ... and my mental health suffered because of it.

I am a disciplined and strong-willed person – that's what has got me so far in life – but at that point I felt like my problems were insurmountable. Still, I only knew one way to deal with difficulty, and that was to lean on faith. For an extended period of time, I was in an emotional and spiritual tug of war with God. All through recovery, taking yet more pain medicine, maintaining my work commitments, and while still coming to terms with the "foreverness" of my chronic illness, I relied on my family to an extent that we had not experienced before. The closeness to and dependence on other human beings to keep myself healthy was profoundly humbling.

During this time, I gained a new perspective on the platitudes that Christians share when the conversation about health and healing comes up. We are quick to say, "Just pray about it" without further thought. People rarely spend time really listening to what's happening with a sick person, finding out what their state of mind is, sitting with them while they process their pain, whatever it may look like.

What we should all be doing is taking stock of our words and thinking about whether we are being helpful or harmful. Sometimes it's not about sharing your own story, because that won't necessarily make someone feel better. Sometimes it's about sharing in the human experience and simply being present for the other person, something that my family did for me in ways I could not have imagined.

God says, "For I know the plans I have for you, plans to prosper you and not to harm you, plans to give you hope and a future" (Jeremiah 29:11), but during that time I started to lose sight of that future. I had no idea what each new day would be like and I was largely just going through the motions.

When we spoke about it all, after the initial period of shock and readjustment had passed, my mother told me she believed I was depressed at the time. It was a time during which my faith, my self-esteem and my mental health took serious knocks. I had to draw on all the strength I had inside me and hold on tighter to God. I had to believe in that prosperous future because no matter how confused or scared I was, I knew one thing stayed true: that God was by my side.

I have come out on the other side with a clearer, stronger perspective on my faith – what it really means to *have faith* – and my relationship with God in its fullness.

By God's grace, I have continued to live a full life that allows me to express my talents, reach new goals and, above all, share the Gospel with everyone I connect with. In the story of my life, illness is not a full stop.

My greatest love story

I met the love of my life in primary school.

At the age of nine or ten, I was settling into my school career, developing my interests and starting to strengthen some friendships. I had a small clique and we moved around together; even at that age I was popular and extroverted, and I attracted kids who knew what was cool. When I met Eva, she was friends with two other girls, and one named Gloria was her closest friend. I stole Eva from Gloria, actually.

Gloria's parents and mine knew each other, so the two of us had a friendship, and through Gloria, I met Eva. I was drawn to her – she was outspoken and full of energy, just like me – and we grew closer and closer. In Grade 6, as precocious preteens, we took our friendship to the next level: we decided to be each other's best friend. From then on, we were inseparable; you wouldn't see one of us without the other. We were together in everything, excelling side by side in academics, and later becoming competitive debaters together; we did very well in sports, too – she in netball and I in hockey – and we held each other up all the way into high school.

Eva and I complemented each other in every way that mattered. In no time she went from a best friend to a sister, to something akin to a soulmate. My mother, who was as strict as any other Christian parent in the nineties, did not allow sleepovers. Yet, Eva was always over at our house. She became an extension of me, of my life.

We went to church together. Or, more accurately, I moved over to her church so that we could be in the arts and culture department together. We had to be together: Monday to Friday at school was not enough, Saturday was not enough – we had to have Sunday, too!

There was no family gathering of hers that I was not a part of, and she knew my family very well, too. Eva and I would take up space wherever we were, these two short, light-skinned, loud girls, laughing and clowning around. We could be ourselves fully and never worry that one would outshine the other.

We successfully did life together, from primary school to high school, through varsity and beyond into the years of adulting. There are no memories that don't include her. There's this joke that goes, "You know you are really best friends with someone if there are no proper pictures of the two of you". For Eva and me, there were no posed photo opportunities and we were often too busy with one thing or the other to even remember to take out the camera. Any photos of us that do exist show how animated we always were: we're mid-sentence or in the middle of some demonstration (because somehow we were always the centre of attention) or sharing big laughs.

She was by my side while I found my feet in the entertainment industry; I watched her become a doctor. At milestones, like my first property or my first car, she was there. When times were tough, she was there. When she was getting married and she asked me to be her maid of honour, I was there.

Eva and I could talk honestly about any- and everything. And when we fought? It was fierce. It was the kind of arguing and expression of disappointment that you could only have with someone you loved with your whole heart and soul. And it could get petty, too: I remember she would grumble about me not having time for her "because I'm with my other friends". It's the kind of jealousy that comes from a friend who values you so highly that they can't imagine not being part of all areas of your life.

But the thing about life is that it expands and it becomes full – of tasks, responsibilities, distractions. Eva and I were tightly bonded, but we were not immune to those changing tides of life. I remember we had an extended rough patch a few years out of varsity. We didn't talk for many months. When we came back together and talked through all our frustrations, expectations, hopes and fears for each other and our friendship, it was so beautiful. I could see how much we had grown as people and, more importantly, how desperate we still were to be there for each other, to live our lives together.

Our love for each other was clear as crystal to everyone around us and even spilled over onto social media, where Eva would often write captions calling me her "smile keeper". She would write about how much she loved me and I would do the same for my best friend. We would display this big sisterhood, this incredible love that, from the outside, had no explanation. We would go to the ends of the earth for each other. We always knew exactly where we stood with each other.

I look at my friendships now and, while I love all my people dearly, none of the relationships come close to what I had with Eva.

At this point, one year after her passing, I am still struggling to process the fact that she's no longer here. Many times, I have caught myself dialling her phone number to ask her advice or tell her what's going on in my day. I have found myself saying out loud, in the middle of conversations, "Eva is gone, you know?" I have to keep reminding myself.

When I got the phone call letting me know that Eva had passed on, I collapsed. My world broke down and I have still not recovered.

Eva and I were Jesus girls. We loved our God and lived out our faith together. So naturally, when this huge thing happened, I turned to Scripture. All the common verses about death and grief that people share, the platitudes that are supposed to get people through the pain, took on a different colour for me. It was now personal, and it prompted me to examine my faith.

In John 11:25-26, the Bible says: "Jesus said to her, 'I am the resurrection and the life. The one who believes in me will live, even though they die; and whoever lives by believing in me will never die. Do you believe this?'"

The Lord promises us eternal life and I knew that part of Scripture well. As Christians, we know that a physical death is not the end because our souls go on to heaven, where we will live by God's side for eternity. Still, when death comes to take someone we love, we feel that loss deeply, and we can fixate on that pain.

I absolutely fell into a depression after Eva died. Each day when I remembered that she wasn't there, I had to also remind myself that yes, *I believe*. Like in John 11:26, I believe that those who live believing in Jesus and His promise of eternal life will indeed not die, even though their bodies pass away.

Accepting that truth, but also having the reality of standing by her casket, and going to her gravesite, and never being able to touch or talk to her again, is incredibly painful. There is this conflict in my heart every day. Still, my resounding answer to the question in John 11:26 is "Yes" – and I pray every day to renew that yes.

Knowing that the souls of those who believe will be given a place in heaven also encouraged me to think differently about another well-known part of Scripture, Psalm 116:15 (KJV), which says, "Precious in the sight of the LORD is the death of his faithful servants". Eva was indeed one of the Lord's faithful servants, and it is wonderful to think that He regarded her as "precious".

I still feel that devastation of losing my life's biggest love, and for some time immediately after her passing I was physically unwell. During the time of her funeral, my sister Bokang came to me and told me, "I can see you holding your breath". She patted me hard in the middle of my chest to jolt me out of my stupor. I could not breathe, thinking about how Eva was gone. This was more than heartbreak.

As I spent more time trying to understand what was happening, I came to another popular grief-related verse.

Psalm 34:18 tells us, "The Lord is close to the broken-hearted, and saves those who are crushed in spirit."

I have always been familiar with the first part, but it is that second part – He *saves* those who are crushed in spirit – that was highlighted for me. I had been sad before, I had been in pain before, things had happened that had broken my heart. But this? Eva's death? It crushed my spirit. I was unable to go on. I needed that saving. I was not far from God or keeping my distance from Him; I was not turning away, saying, "I'm not going to talk to Him". I was still going to church, still participating, still having faith – still seeking God's face – but my spirit was crushed and I needed to be saved. I had to acknowledge that.

It was comforting. But admittedly on some days I would think, "But why did my spirit have to be crushed in the first place?"

Yet I was also aware that being saved from that place of a crushed spirit did not mean that the pain would magically go away. But while it was still there, I could cling to God and trust that He would save me.

This is also how I have seen God amplified during my time of inexplicable grief. Having to turn to His Word to see clearly through this path has made God the touchpoint through it all.

At first, I thought that God was distracting me from the pain by keeping me busy. I mean, weeks after Eva's funeral, the journey with *Jesus This, Jesus That* began. Every day, the Lord kept His name in my mouth and on my mind. I had this desire to listen to God's voice and do what He was telling me to.

The voice of God was the only clear thing; He was amplified through the confusion, grief and pain. It was almost unbelievable how fully God was revealing Himself to me at a time like that.

It was not a distraction, but it was a reassurance, an affirmation that God loved me. Through *Jesus This, Jesus That* and the weekly Bible studies I started to lead, I realise now that God was using me to minister to people while also ministering to me. The verses and sermons I shared were healing me even as they opened the hearts of people who would tune in. God was showing me that He will always be there for me. He became the only thing I could see, just like it is described in Isaiah 6:1: "… I saw the Lord, high and exalted …" He was in front of my eyes and in my heart and in my speech. I was crushed in spirit but I had the promise that I would be saved.

I lost the greatest love of my life, a once-in-a-lifetime friend, confidante and sister. The person I would laugh with, plan with, pray with, and dream with. Eva meant so much to so many people, and she had so much more to do.

Her passing has impressed upon me how urgent life is. Eva and I lived so much life together in a short space of time – growing up, travelling together, developing our faith together. In the time since she has been gone, I have been learning that how I spend my time matters more than anything. I have been consciously, intentionally watching the quality of my interactions, of the time I spend with my people. Time is the most precious thing I can give them, and I see that now more than ever.

As for my journey with grief: I am not completely okay and I don't know if or when I ever will be. I have never experienced this before. But I will say that I am aware of and I am grateful for how this experience of grief is strengthening my faith in God.

Say what you mean

For Christians, there is the important commitment to "walking the talk", that is, being true to God and His teaching through your speech.

Words are powerful. As the Bible says, there is power in the tongue – and we have the responsibility to speak truth and life. Your speech must be impeccable.

A practical way to apply this is to refer to Proverbs 3:3-4, which says, "Let love and faithfulness never leave you; bind them around your neck, write them on the tablet of your heart. Then you will win favour and a good name in the sight of God and man." (the New Century Version reads, "Wear them like a necklace ...") This means that kindness and compassion should be the first things people see and experience when they encounter you. There should be no doubt who you represent when you speak, and your actions should match your words.

In this way you can carry out the responsibility, as set out in 1 Timothy 4:12, to be pure in your speech.

An example of when I was challenged on the level of speech is the panel discussion I was asked to be a part of for Castle Milk Stout. In a conversation about spirituality, which the other guests had contributed to throughout the hour, I found myself in a confrontation with a public figure known as Bishop Joshua Maponga. He questioned Christian faith in God in general, displaying a bias towards African spirituality (what could also be called Traditional African Religion) and saying that the routinised practice of churchgoing and Christianity was the behaviour of "schizophrenics".

On a show that was produced to open up difficult conversations, where people were already becoming heated and struggling with having their beliefs questioned, the personal stakes were high and the bishop's words could easily have set me off. However, by grace and because I have been cultivating my faith journey for so many years, I was able to keep my speech respectful and respectable.

I said to everyone: I know my faith, I have my real experience with Jesus Christ, and that is where I find my spiritual practice.

Equally, I don't give myself the right to judge people's choices: I stand strong enough in my Christianity to talk about and gain general knowledge on different religions and practices, but in order to keep myself in line and to keep my boundaries, I don't speak on things when I don't have the authority to do so. I rely on the Word and not on discriminatory or judgemental behaviours. As the Lord says in Jeremiah 1:7-8: "Do not say, 'I am too young.' You must go to everyone I send you to and say whatever I command you. Do not be afraid of them, for I am with you and will rescue you."

And that is the essence of it: speech is kept pure through obedience, which is cultivated through a close relationship with God. God is the one who can affirm you and give you the ability to speak in a way that sets the example that Paul speaks about in 1 Timothy 4:12.

There is a security that comes with having a close relationship with God, and that is what gives us the confidence needed to speak and speak well. Through God, we can carry out all the good work that we read about in the Bible.

The conversation on that show spilled over, as it would, onto social media. There it branched out to many other areas and ultimately took on a different shape and tone. But what I took from that experience was that the people who were listening in and who heard me speak understood where I was coming from, and some commended the way I spoke with clarity and discipline. On social media, that's a rare occurrence. Usually, the conversations are quick to get out of hand and even things said in good faith can be taken out of context in a terrible way. But again, that's where the reminder to keep your conduct and your speech pure comes in.

I have found that, as much as I enjoy a parasocial relationship with the followers on my page, I have to be strict about what I say and who I interact with. In this way I can keep myself accountable. A few times a year, sites like Instagram and X (formerly known as Twitter) have a trending topic that sends everyone's fingers into a typing frenzy. It's the kind of thing that one could easily get caught up in.

Often people will seek out the opinions of public figures and then use those as their guide in place of forming their own thoughts. With this in mind and with the constant intent to honour God with my speech and conduct, I have learned how to navigate difficult social media spaces.

I take guidance from 2 Timothy 2, which builds on the instruction we find in 1 Timothy 4, to guard one's speech. 2 Timothy 2:15 says: "Do your best to present yourself to God as one approved, a worker who does not need to be ashamed and who correctly handles the word of truth." And 2 Timothy 2:25 says: "Opponents must be gently instructed, in the hope that God will grant them repentance leading them to a knowledge of the truth …". Taken together, they speak about immersing yourself in the Word of God so that when you speak, the truth is the first thing people hear, and it positively influences them.

It is about how to approach communicating with and preaching to people, and it is also a reminder about how seriously speech must be taken. Importantly, Christians should not speak to sound better or make themselves look important. It is about teaching people about God and changing their perspective of Him, not of yourself.

Above all, I know that I have the responsibility to be an example to believers and to everyone I connect with. It's a responsibility I take seriously and with pride.

Go out boldly
with faith

In the Bible, the disciples were people who Jesus chose to be examples. He chose them to be close to Him, to live with Him and learn from Him. They had exclusive access to the source. When it was time for them to leave Jesus, He told them to go to the ends of the world, baptise people in the name of the Father, the Son and the Holy Spirit, and to teach those they find to obey everything that Jesus had taught the disciples – to be examples going out to influence more people in the ways of the Lord, to win more souls for heaven.

Now, as He did then, God is calling us to focus on how our lives look – in faith, purity, love, conduct, speech – and to polish them up and get them right, so that we can be the example that He knows we have the potential to be.

The big work of building the Lord's Kingdom starts with the details of everyday life. Every. Day. There are requirements – clear, non-negotiable – that you must meet. Knowing and accepting this puts you on the right footing for life.

Going to the ends of the world means reaching out to colleagues, neighbours, family members, the people you share your daily commute with. Everywhere you look, there's someone who you could potentially influence with your speech, conduct, faith, love and purity.

The work of sharing the Gospel can be intimidating, and it is very serious, but here's the thing: it is not unattainable. Through studying Scripture like 1 Timothy 4:12, which has guided us to this point in the book, we spend time with God, drawing confidence from our relationship with Him, and that confidence is what confirms that all the promises God makes to His people are within reach, that they *are* attainable.

This is what I want you to remember: keep going back to the Word. Make it your personal quest. Think about it and say, "Lord, I want you to use me, I want to be part of the bigger plan."

In your efforts to become stronger in your faith, take time to ask yourself what you truly believe, what you stand for.

At a certain point, I had to ask myself that question and evaluate what my faith journey was based on. I grew up in the church, I know how it works, I know how to make declarations of faith. But what I have learned is that my relationship with God has to be completely personal. *I* have to consciously decide to pursue Him, to believe in Him, to take up the responsibility to represent Him. I have to get real about how well I am conducting my relationship with Him.

Once I started reading 1 Timothy 4:12 and internalising it, I turned a new page in my book with God and started working more diligently to align all my time and actions on earth to His purpose for me.

In every way, the focus is on God. That is my source of strength, courage and comfort. In writing these stories I have been reminded over and over that I have the grace of God over my life. What I have survived, achieved, overcome, learned, what I would like to see in my future – these are all protected by His grace. I have confidence in that because I have spent time getting closer and closer to Him, intentionally going back to the Word, using it as my essential guide through life.

My wish is that you would start doing the same, today. Now is the time to ask yourself how you love, how you live your faith, how people experience you, how you sound, how you are upholding purity. Draw nearer to the Lord and ask Him to help you answer these questions and get on the right track.

Look at your stories, look at your life. Do you see how God has had His hand on you? Are you looking for a faith refresh? Which of the five pillars of Christian life do you need to work on?

Once you have looked at your life through this new lens, use that same honesty and intention to steel yourself to ask the next question: Are you ready to align your behaviour to the Word of God in order to take on the work of changing this cold, corrupt, evil world? To pierce through the chaos and make an impact, you must be willing to fix the five pillars and go forth boldly, knowing your mission.

1 Timothy 4:12 is, in my view, the blueprint for this mission. Everything you need to align with is in there. The even better news is that all the pillars that are laid out by Paul in that passage are explained beautifully in other passages throughout the Bible. You don't have to walk in faith alone – God's Word lays it all out for you.

Throughout the book, passages from the Bible are quoted or referred to in service of a greater point. It can be difficult to retain this information after one reading, so this is a space that you can use to reflect. Think about what you know, what you want to learn, and where you want to go.

❧ What do you believe?

❧ Who are your accountability partners? I speak about community in the stories I tell. Who is your faith community, holding you up on your journey?

🌿 Which of the five tenets in 1 Timothy 4:12 do you believe you can improve on?

🌿 Which of the five tenets in 1 Timothy 4:12 would you say you have placed emphasis on? We often lean on what we believe we are good at, and ignore the other areas we could be putting energy into.

🌿 What does quality time with God and the Word look like to you?

🌿 How have you been exercising faith in your daily life? That is: Where are you quick to apply faith? Which areas of your life do you find yourself *not* believing God for guidance and grace?

Use these questions to make notes and plans for strengthening your relationship with God and realigning your path with Him, today.

My wish for you, the reader

My desire for you, and for myself, is that we may continue to hear God for ourselves, and to hear God for our generation. I think that is the perfect example of a disciple: one who seeks relationship with God, and communion and fellowship with Him; and one who is able to hear God for the generation in which God has allowed them to exist.

The responsibility of walking out your life with God, even in private, is such a beautiful journey, but it must be intentional. Being a disciple means stepping out for the world to see and hear you decree and declare that Jesus Christ is Lord! Let it be clear in the way that you live your life, in the way that you talk, in the way that you present yourself, and in the way that you live out your salvation.

After putting the stories in this book together, and as I continue to examine my own faith and my own relationship with God, I have found myself dwelling on Romans 8:31-39 (NLT), which says:

What shall we say about such wonderful things as these? If God is for us, who can ever be against us? Since he did not spare even his own Son but gave him up for us all, won't he also give us everything else? Who dares accuse us whom God has chosen for his own? No one – for God himself has given us right standing with himself. Who then will condemn us? No one – for Christ Jesus died for us and was raised to life for us, and he is sitting in the place of honour at God's right hand, pleading for us. Can anything ever separate us from Christ's love? Does it mean he no longer loves us if we have trouble or calamity, or are persecuted, or hungry, or destitute, or in danger, or threatened with death? (As the Scriptures say, "For your sake we are killed every day; we are being slaughtered like sheep.") No, despite all these things, overwhelming victory is ours through Christ, who loved us. And I am convinced that nothing can ever separate us from God's love. Neither death nor life, neither angels nor demons, neither our fears for today nor our worries about tomorrow – not even the powers of hell can separate us from God's love. No power in the sky above or in the earth below – indeed, nothing in all creation will ever be able to separate us from the love of God that is revealed in Christ Jesus our Lord.

In the past, I have looked at this part of Scripture and thought of warfare and fighting against powers and principalities, but now when I read that first verse – "What shall we say …?" – I stop and think to myself, "God, You have been *good*. What can I say about the wonderful things that You have done? About my walk with You, how You've covered me, protected me, forgiven me, had mercy on me? You've walked me through this life journey." Then I think of the next part, "If God is for us, who can ever be against us?"

Here we tend to think of external factors, people or things outside of ourselves that we have to fend off. But I see now that I should rather be thinking, "What part of my conduct counts against me living my best life for God? What in my speech could be against me? What impurities could be a hurdle? What lack of faith could be in the way of me living a fully expressed life with Christ? And the fact that God loves me so much that even those things can't stand against me?" This is the value of this Scripture to me now.

When it goes on in verse 32 to say, "Since he did not spare even his own Son but gave him up for us all, won't he also give us everything else?", I am reminded that God was able to give us Jesus. He wants me to have a good life – and not good in terms of material things, but a holistic, holy, quality life – and He has no intention of withholding those good things from me. Why should I worry? Why should I backslide? Why should my conduct not reflect Him? Why should my faith not reflect Him? Why should my speech not reflect Him? God first loved me and that's why I'm able to boldly love.

I am not a disciple because I'm a good person. I'm not a disciple because I am "worthy". I'm not a disciple because I have a special anointing that sets me apart. I am a disciple because God has chosen me as His own: "Who dares accuse us whom God has chosen for his own?" This alone freed me from the burden of thinking that I'm doing this on my own strength, and prompted me to focus on resting in the fact that God *chose* me. He chose me. I don't know why He chose me; I can't come up with logical reasons why He chose me, but I choose to rest in the knowledge and hope that I am chosen by God.

The passage in Romans continues to tell us, "… for God himself has given us right standing with himself." I have right standing with God; no one gets to decide that but Him. Again, it's so freeing to know that God loves me that much.

Then we come to the part that we all love as Christians, verse 35: Can anything ever separate us from Christ's love? And I just want us to sit there for a little. What is it that can separate us from God's love? Nothing. The Bible tells us: Nothing. So that is what being a disciple means for me today, and I pray it means the same for you as you journey in your Christian walk. To be known, to be loved, to be seen by God means to be a disciple, and what is beautiful about being a disciple is that God sends us out to do His work.

My latest realisation about the true meaning of discipleship came to me when I examined the actual meaning of the phrase, "God is using you." I used to think of the Kingdom work in my life as God using me: the kindness I am able to extend to people, the connections I have been making with *Jesus This, Jesus That*, following my mother's example of loving people and bringing them close to me so that I can make a difference in their lives, everything that my family and I have been through together – I used to think of that as God using us.

Now I realise that in helping people, in serving, in standing in faith, in watching my conduct, in pursuing purity and holiness, in living out my faith – that has not been God using me. All the experiences and different accounts that I have shared throughout the book are an expression that God has not been using me – but God has been *loving* me.

Anything that is used comes to a point where it becomes unuseful, a point where you have overused it.

But God's love is everlasting and endures forever. Me serving, loving, pursuing holiness, faith, purity in conduct and speech are me expressing my love to God, because He first loved me. So, God is not using me, God is loving me. God is not using me; I'm His child: He's loving me. The expression of the love that He showers on me is the transformation of the way I behave. The way I see the world and my desires for my life are slowly but steadily transformed, and my life begins to reflect God's heart. I am a disciple because I am loved.

A lot of the things that we want to do for God, the work we want to do in His name, requires us to have a full relationship with Him. That's where it all begins. That's what set the disciples apart from the many great men and women in the Bible: the fact that they walked with Christ. They lived and worked alongside Him. David, for example, did amazing things; so did Moses and Joseph and Esther. The list of great men and women who did incredible work in the Bible is long; they all lived out their faith beautifully, standing up for God.

Yet the disciples are different because they were set apart; they were chosen to have a personal relationship with Jesus, to sit at His feet and learn from Him. The disciples in the Bible had a front-row seat to the work and teachings of Jesus. They were in relationship with Him on a very special, very close level.

My desire is that, above all things, before wanting to *be* anything for God, we would all be *for* Him, and pursue Him; intentionally pursue relationship with Him.

Jesus spent a significant time of His ministry discipling the disciples – that is, teaching and walking with them through life, and revealing to them the mysteries of the Kingdom of God, so that when He sent them out, He was confident in their abilities to continue the good work.

In Matthew 28:19-20, Jesus says to the disciples: "Therefore go and make disciples of all nations, baptising them in the name of the Father and of the Son and of the Holy Spirit, and teaching them to obey everything I have commanded you. And surely I am with you always, to the very end of the age."

After their time learning and living beside Jesus, the disciples were given full permission to go out and share the Gospel.

Jesus said they should go and teach everything that He had told them, and teach others to obey Jesus, and the disciples should do this strictly, following what Jesus had done. In this I see that Jesus made it clear what a disciple was meant to do: disciples go out and teach, not from their personal opinion or emotional judgements, or from what they can work out for themselves, but straight from the source of knowledge, which is Jesus Christ.

I want to encourage you to take time and be intentional about your walk and your relationship with God, so that you will not be swayed by circumstances. I pray that your love for Him may be rooted in relationship and in knowing Him, and that within the relationship blossoms an opportunity for us to stand up for Him boldly in the world through conduct, through speech, through faith, through purity.

My parting words to you are: Pursue Him. Once you consciously and intentionally make the decision to pursue Jesus Christ, then the mandate comes, then the purpose comes, then the vehicle for the purpose comes. Everything comes out of knowing and pursuing and living for God.

And remember that you must pursue God above your pursuit of doing good deeds or living a righteous life; you must keep God at the centre, and then all the actions and answers will follow. Do not try to lean on your own understanding of what a relationship with God should look like, or what it will yield.

Above all things, may He truly be our personal Lord – meaning we yield and submit to Him – and Saviour, meaning we know that we fall short of His glory, yet we are called righteous because He is righteous.

Acknowledgements

Well, here we are.

Since I first piped up and said that I loved to write, everyone has said, "You should write a book!"

To the Grade 6 version of me who took that to heart and wrote her first novel in between exams, then threw the "manuscript" away and hasn't stopped thinking about it since: here's our second attempt. I hope you like it.

It all started with really giving myself over to reading and to books, so I would like to thank my father, Thulani Manabe, for encouraging – and funding! – my voracious reading habits since I was a child. Thank you for showing me that in libraries and bookshops I could find many worlds of opportunity and live a thousand different lives.

To every teacher who called on me to read aloud, pushed me along with helpful remarks and otherwise made the world of words a welcoming, exciting and inspiring one: thank you!

I am grateful to all the authors who have trusted me to develop their stories and edit them into books that the world needs.

When Susan Jordaan of Lux Verbi first contacted me about collaborating with Rorisang Thandekiso on a book, I was surprised, but determined to take on a new challenge. I was in a bit of a professional lull and I was eager to redirect my energy into something productive.

As I began to interview Rorisang and write her story, and the project started to take shape, I was terrified: What had I got myself into?

In moments when I doubted my ability to write a book, I thought about how an opportunity like this one would not have come along my path if I had not already proven I was capable of handling it, if someone hadn't recognised something in me. So, I would like to sincerely thank Efemia Chela and Mbali Sikakana for passing my name on to the right desk.

Efemia, your sharp wit, sense of humour and deep investment in the craft of editing and publishing keep me sane whenever I start to wonder whether books, which I love so much, love me back.

To my sister, Busisiwe Matshonyonge, who always excited to hear my latest updates on the project and whose faith in me and my work has never wavered: I can't thank you enough for all your love and support!

To Pearl Pillay, the constant in my life: thank you for all the ways, big and small, that you support my vision for my life and encourage me to make bold decisions – even when I would much rather stay in my corner and mind my own business. I am so glad our lives are intertwined.

To Rorisang: I am so deeply appreciative of how you opened up your life to me and allowed your story to pour forth onto these pages. I hope you are as proud of what we have done as I am. Thank you for your time, and thank you to your family for lending you to me.

To Sthe: thank you for finding all the gaps in Rorisang's schedule: we would have been lost without you!

Thank you, Susan, for trusting me with this. I sensed your confidence in me and did my best not to let you down. I hope I've been one of your best gambles yet!

NKHENSANI MANABE

www.ingramcontent.com/pod-product-compliance
Lightning Source LLC
Chambersburg PA
CBHW031130090426
42738CB00008B/1034